NICK BROOMFIELD

of related interest from Faber and Faber
IMAGINING REALITY
THE FABER BOOK OF DOCUMENTARY
Edited by
Kevin Macdonald and Mark Cousins

NICK BROOMFIELD

Documenting Icons

Edited by Jason Wood

faber and faber

First published in 2005
by Faber and Faber Limited
3 Queen Square London WC1N 3AU

Typeset in Sabon by Faber and Faber Ltd
Printed in England by

A CIP record for this book
is available from the British Library

All images within the book, except marked otherwise,
by Nick Broomfield

ISBN 0-571-22624-8

2 4 6 8 10 9 7 5 3 1

Contents

Acknowledgements

Jason Wood

I would first and foremost like to express my appreciation to Nick Broomfield for his full and dedicated co-operation with this project. He was a most generous host as well as an honest interviewee, and I greatly enjoyed the time we spent together during the writing of this book, though I could have done without the savage thrashings he administered during our numerous post-interview games of table tennis.

I should also like to thank Jo Harkins at Lafayette Films for providing me with tapes and source materials; Elizabeth Wood of DocHouse for her fascinating insights into all matters documentary-related; and both City Screen and The OTHER Cinema (especially Melanie Crawley) for facilitating a Nick Broomfield retrospective that set this book in motion. Michael Leake was characteristically helpful in data storage, and Daniel Graham assisted with a number of the transcriptions. Colin Young was a valuable fact-checking facility. And honourable mentions are also extended to Barney Broomfield, Emily Bruni and Jez Lewis.

At Faber, I would like to thank Walter Donohue and Richard T. Kelly for their patience, advice and general willingness to follow this book through to completion.

Finally, I am again indebted to my wife and family for their support, encouragement and numerous sacrifices during the undertaking of yet another writing assignment.

By way of thanks for all his encouragement, I dedicate this book to Andi Engel.

Nick Broomfield

A special thank you to Charles Finch for making fantastic deals. Shani Hinton and Peter Dally for legal help at all times, Riete Oord and Barry Ackroyd for their wonderful work on *The Leader, Aileen, Too White for Me* and *Tracking Down Maggie*, Peter Dale (*Biggie and Tupac*) for his help and support, Nick Fraser (*Kurt and Courtney*) against overwhelming odds, Michael Jackson, Peter Moore, Shelia Nevins, Nancy Abraham, Barry Gavin, Sir Arthur Elton, Bruce Beresford, Bernice Rubens, Kahanne corn, Richard Lewis, Jo Human, Mr Cahoun, Colin Young, Joan Churchill, Claire Fergusoon, Barney Broomfield, Jo Harkins, and Michele D'acosta all of whom made an enormous contribution to the films, and without whose input, they could not have been made.

Introduction

I'm relatively sure that Nick Broomfield needs little by way of an introduction, and I would hope that everything that you need to know about him and his work can be found in the following pages. My first experience of one of our foremost documentary film-makers came whilst watching *The Leader, His Driver and the Driver's Wife* when it was initially broadcast on British television. It was, for me, an epochal moment, opening my eyes to the power of the documentary format to inform us of worlds, figures and ideologies previously unknown. It also revealed that documentary could be a source of entertainment as well as a learning tool – something that Broomfield himself is keen to stress – and I recall watching transfixed as this slight-looking Englishman with a rather posh accent enraged the fearsome, thuggish and decidedly bulky right-wing Afrikaner leader Eugene Terre'Blanche by deliberately turning up late for an already oft-postponed interview, rubbing salt in the wound by offering that 'going for some tea' had been the reason for his delayed arrival. I later learned this to be one of Broomfield's 'elephant traps', a tried and trusted documentary technique that the London-born director would intermittently employ throughout his career (and which would later come to exert a sizeable influence on *Bowling for Columbine* [2002] and *Fahrenheit 9/11* [2004] by the polemicist Michael Moore.)

Mention of Moore invariably prompts the drawing of parallels with Broomfield, and the Bush-baiting director is certainly the most recent – and high-profile – figure to have been profoundly influenced by Broomfield's pioneering work. The phenomenal box-office success Moore has enjoyed has undoubtedly been a contributing factor to the current renaissance in documentary film-making and the fact that the form, once considered to be relatively specialized and a theatrical anomaly, is now increasingly available on cinema screens. Aggressively marketed and released on multiple prints, *Touching the Void* (2003), *Capturing the Friedmans* (2003), *Super Size Me* (2004), *The Story of the Weeping Camel* (2003) and *Spellbound* (2002) are just a few examples of this phenomenon. Amongst all this – and the current popularity of documentary is undoubtedly one of the factors that makes a book on one of its most celebrated and visible practitioners so timely – it is worth remembering that Broomfield was one of the first directors to think about his films as theatrical entities as opposed to purely televisual ones. Of course, D. A. Pennebaker's seminal *Don't Look Back* (1967) was also conceived for cinema (and Pennebaker, alongside Frederick Wiseman and Broomfield's National Film School professor Colin Young, is one of three figures Broomfield cites as exerting a profound influence over his own work). But Broomfield, even at the time of early films such as *Who Cares, Proud to Be British* and *Behind the Rent Strike*, consistently argued that his films should play on big screens and be seen by as wide an audience as possible.

Alongside the creative and commercial renaissance of the documentary and the pivotal role Broomfield has played in this, the other spur for this book was the UK release of Broomfield's recent work *Aileen: The Life and Death of a Serial Killer* (2003) and the corresponding Nick Broomfield retrospective which I programmed at The OTHER Cinema in London. Whilst rewatching the twenty-four films that Broomfield has made to date, what immediately became apparent was that as a body of work the films were tremendously varied in style and execution.

From *Who Cares* (1971) onwards, Broomfield has explored every documentary aesthetic, adopting whatever approach best suits the subject. There is an overriding sense that, in general, style should be subservient to content; but it is also clear that the approach should also replicate Broomfield's personal experience of completing the film, the director himself being of the mind that the films frequently serve as personal diaries. Thus we run the gamut from observational cinema or *cinema vérité* through to the film-maker-as-mirror of the ever-shifting environment in which he happens to be working. This was taken to its logical conclusion in *Driving Me Crazy* (1988), a pivotal work in which Broomfield quite painfully but with delicious humour – a frequent and invariably overlooked facet of the director's output – documents the collapse of the very film he is making. Self-confessedly indebted to films such as Michael Rubbo's *Waiting for Fidel* (1974) and Ross McElwee's *Sherman's March* (1986), *Driving Me Crazy* employed the technique to innovative and idiosyncratic effect. In many ways the technique would frequently recur throughout Broomfield's work, becoming the director's way of dealing with the iconic and invariably unwilling figures he was attempting to interview. Though apt to pursue his quarry doggedly, Broomfield was equally happy to make a film about their unwillingness to be interviewed on camera, as became the case with the aforementioned *The Leader, His Driver* and also with *Tracking Down Maggie* (1994), a film that uncovers ex-prime minister Margaret Thatcher's nefarious and nepotistic arms activities, and a personal/political portrait on which, one may hope, the ruinous legacy of the 'Iron Lady' shall come to rest.

It is this approach – one that frequently necessitates Broomfield appearing on camera, a technique that the subsequent pages of this book also reveal to be a recurring contractual obligation – that has seen the director chastised by his detractors for becoming the film's subject or central focus. I feel such criticisms to be entirely misplaced, ignoring as they do both the aforementioned desire that the work should replicate the conditions in which the film was made and, perhaps more pertinently, the extraordinary range of pressing subjects with which Broomfield's work deals. As with the Thatcher film, politics, and particularly how political actions and institutions reflect upon ordinary and underprivileged people, play a major role in Broomfield's work.

There are other increasingly socially relevant or resonant themes to which the director continually returns, often under the guise of a portrait of an iconic individual. Thus *Heidi Fleiss: Hollywood Madam* (1995) becomes an exposé of Hollywood mores; *Kurt and Courtney* (1997) an examination of the destructive power of corporate America, local economic depression and freedom of speech; *Biggie and Tupac* (2002) begins as a look at hip-hop rivalry but emerges as Chandleresque indictment of racism and LAPD corruption; whilst Broomfield's two films on executed 'serial' killer Aileen Wuornos are powerful portraits of the American justice system and the commercialization of crime, as well as powerful anti-death penalty statements, offering sympathy to a character most others were quick to shun and condemn. Broomfield's compassion towards his subjects is another consistent thread, running from Ethel Singleton in *Behind the Rent Strike* (1973) through the likes of *Juvenile Liaison*'s (1976) Sergeant Rey, the recruits of *Soldier Girls* (1980), and their deeply scarred leader, Sergeant Abing. There is even an attempt to understand the actions of Courtney Love by documenting the loveless environment in which she grew up. These are all subjects and issues that powerfully impinge upon all our worlds.

In closing, I return to Nick's desire that his films should reflect their subjects, and his own experience – for good or for ill – of documenting them. This is an approach that I have also tried to apply to the following text, and I hope that it covers the film-maker's frequently self-deprecating humour, his understanding of and love for his craft, and the traditions of documentary film-making. I also hope that this book is reflective of a fierce, extremely perceptive and ever-questioning intelligence, coupled with a genuine interest in people. I had great fun writing this book and interviewing Nick over numerous meetings; I would sincerely hope that something of this comes across too.

I

Broomfield and Son 1

Beginnings, Who Cares, The National Film School,
Proud to Be British, Behind the Rent Strike

© Maurice Broomfield

Roller-bearing

JW: *I wanted to begin by talking a little bit about your background and the influence of your photographer father, Maurice.*[1]

NB: My father was a very big influence, and I think that growing up with his images certainly affected me on a subconscious level, even if not directly. The thing that really affected me about my father was that he was a very technical photographer, although he never studied photography or went to the equivalent of a photographic school. He is, in fact, a very technical person, and this is quite unlike me. He started his working life in factories; his first job was making copper pipes to a certain diameter in a Rolls Royce factory and, in a way, his heart was always in industry. His father had been a lace designer and was such a great artist that he could even put crinkles in his drawings. When you look at his designs, which were white ink on black card, you would really think that it was a piece of fabric. My father was very much in this tradition, from Derbyshire, everything done with extreme thoroughness and in a very particular way. He was somewhat off-putting to grow up with, because he had such a specific way of doing everything. His photography was a bit like that; he did massive lighting jobs that were very technical. I remember him saying to me that photography is not something where you merely go out and do snaps; it's something that you do for at least a week at a time. That was the kind of discipline he instilled in me.

Probably the biggest single influence was when he took me with him on a job to some lead works in east London down by the Thames. Molten lead was being pressed into sheets, and every time they folded it over an airlock would form in the middle and then there would be an enormous explosion as this was then pressed, and a piece of lead as

3

big as your fist would fly across the factory floor – and this was in the days before people wore helmets. So everyone would crouch down and wince, because they never knew where this piece of lead was going to fly. It was a bit like being in Dante's inferno. All the people that worked in the factory were also an awful green colour because they were dying of lead poisoning. I remember at lunch time my father stopping in his old car by some grassy spot and pulling the roof down – he's a bit of a sun worshipper, like me – and we had some sandwiches. My father is capable of finding beauty everywhere. But I thought this factory was so oppressive and haunting, and realized that I was so lucky not to be there. Up to this point I had done really badly academically and was unruly at school.[2] In fact, I recently sat down with my son Barney and looked at some of the school reports that my father had given me for Christmas, and they were just appalling.

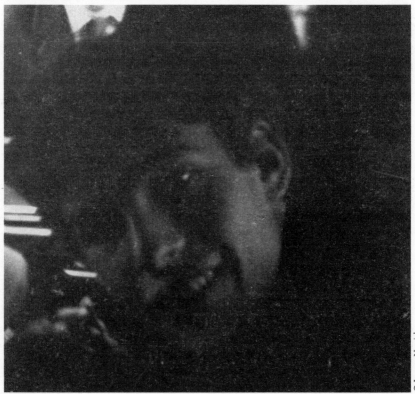

Expelled, the last day of school
June 1965

After I had been expelled from my last school – when I was sixteen or seventeen – my father, who has always been very supportive and very loving, said, 'Now this has gone too far.' He had always wanted me to go to university, but my mother, who was far stricter, really felt that I should go to work now. So I was told that I was going to have to get a job. I remembered the image of this awful lead factory and thought, 'Oh no . . .' For the first time in my life, I began to work really hard. Because of my parents' backgrounds – my father was working-class and my mother was a refugee from Prague – they were always very careful with their money and frugal in their lives, and so I knew that they weren't going to support me financially and that they were serious about this work business. The visit to the factory had also made me very aware that there were people who were nowhere near as fortunate as myself, even though they were probably far more intelligent and capable.

And were you actually interested in your father's work as an art form? Did you pay attention to composition and photography as a way of depicting the reality of people within a specific environment?
I think so, especially with my first film. *Who Cares* was very much a voyage back into the kind of life I could have had if I hadn't bucked up my ideas.

Broomfield's first film, Who Cares, *documents the urban redevelopment of Abercrombie in Liverpool. Later used as evidence at the Royal Commission of Slum Clearance and Re-Housing, the film is a collage of sounds and images that examines the misery inflicted on the working-class communities – communities later destroyed – when they are moved from their terraced accommodation and rehoused in nearby high-rise developments.*

I liked the environment of *Who Cares*. I felt that there was much more of a sense of community, friendship and warmth than there was in the environment that I had grown up in. I always hated middle-class environments with their pettiness and one-upmanship, and I found in those communities in Liverpool a real bonding of people, which I suppose I did come to very much through my father. In a way, it was a search for a life that I might have had. My mother was from a wealthy, intellectual background and we were never really allowed to go back

Rosie and Mabel, *Who Cares*

Johnny Fatso, *Who Cares*

to Derby, where my father had his roots. When we did, it was very stressful. I felt that there was this interesting world back there that I was somehow shut out of; I also felt that there were secrets that I needed to know.

Aesthetically, *Who Cares* was shot almost as a series of stills in black and white and so is, compositionally, very much influenced by my father's work. There's also a nostalgia in that film, a sense of looking for something that you certainly don't get in a more middle-class, propertied environment.

You mentioned that you were unruly at school. Would you describe this as an opposition to authority? It seems to be an attitude that intermittently crops up throughout your work. Peter Moore, your old boss at Channel Four, described you as 'the fly in the ointment'.3
That's exactly who I am, so it's very easy to do it in my films. I don't know exactly why but I always found authority very difficult and I always did very badly in the face of it. I wasn't academic as a child, almost deliberately so. I would start off in the A stream and would then just as quickly find myself in the B stream. My parents tried to correct this by sending me to a really strict prep school, where my performance was even more appalling. There was this tremendous sense of competition to do well and go to the right schools, which also didn't sit comfortably with me. I liked riding around on my bicycle, knocking around with my friends and getting into mischief, so I wasn't going to go for all this stuff, and I hated being shouted at and being told to do things that I didn't want to do.

The prep school I went to was The Hall in Belsize Park – one of the most overachieving schools in the country. Our positions in the class were read out every two weeks in this grand hall with all the parents watching from the galleries; it was rather like something out of Lindsay Anderson's *If* (1968). I was always fourteenth.

How many were there in the class?
Fourteen. In a very stern voice, the master would call your name and then read your position, and I was always fourteenth. One week he made this really cruel joke when he stated that I was sixteenth because two flies had joined up. Of course, everyone screamed with laughter, and I got up and said, 'Screw you,' and ran out of the room in tears. Obviously, I didn't stay at this school for much longer. I found it easier

to be rebellious as opposed to just being squashed. I think that this was also very much to do with the support of my father.

Did experiences such as this also make you more tenacious? Tenacity is an obvious characteristic of your work, especially the later films.
Actually, I don't think that I am particularly tenacious and I certainly don't regard myself as being brave at all.

What about the moment in Kurt and Courtney *when you get up on stage at the American Council of Civil Liberties awards and talk about the journalistic right to exercise freedom of speech?*
Well, I know how much it took me to do that. It was horrific. I don't think I'm naturally brave at all and I often find making my films a little bit of a threatening experience, but I have always promised myself that if I start making a film I will always finish it – no matter what. You often have to push yourself way beyond what you want to do to get there, and this invariably involves persistence. People say that I'm very tenacious with my questions, but I don't necessarily feel that I am. I feel that they are legitimate questions and that I have a right to ask them; there is always a truth behind them. I am someone who hates mountaineering, aqualung diving, any of those extreme activities. And I certainly do things in the course of my work that, left to my own devices, I ordinarily wouldn't do.

Where does the name of your company, Lafayette Films, originate from?
It was a company that my father owned – a portrait business that photographed all the British colonials before they went overseas, so it owned plate-glass negatives of all the colonial administrators. My father acquired this company when he was starting his own portrait business. He was hopelessly unsuccessful at running a portrait business, in the same way that he wasn't as good with the precocious parents of babies as he was with industrial environments. He reached the point where he was ready to sell the company, so, as I liked the name, I simply took it over. It was also a way of carrying on in my father's tradition. I would have called it Broomfield and Son since that sounds like a scrap merchant's . . . and that would also have been especially apt as my son Barney has now started to make his own documentaries.

Would you say that was purely his own choice? Or did you gently steer him in that direction?

He probably didn't have too much of an option having Joan Churchill and I as parents. Joan's father[4] was a very successful educational documentary film-maker. Barney was always surrounded by it. I think it's great. I must also say that it's an incredible life, to find out about the world around you.

Is there also a disadvantage having you and Joan as parents, since Barney's work will invariably now be judged in comparison to yours and Joan's?

I'm obviously slightly biased, but I think that Barney has a really original mind; in fact, I get a lot of my information and ideas from him. It's often this way: the older generation looking to the younger generation for new technical advancements and new ways of seeing things. We also look to them for energy. Barney is undoubtedly very talented. He's making his first film at the moment and stylistically it's influenced by a post-modernist way of looking at things, in the sense that it is often the context and the questions around it that are more interesting than the immediate subject. So his first film is about making his first film.

Sounds Broomfield-esque . . .

It's also quite cunning, because there were plenty of mistakes made on it, but he's managed to incorporate these and they're very funny. He was faced with two choices: he could either go to film school for three years or just dive head first into it and learn by his mistakes. This is basically what you do at film school anyway; at least, that's what I found to be so brilliant during my time at the National Film School. Colin Young was all about people just going out and shooting film and learning about the things that went wrong. Obviously, a film school has to have a lot of money to do that, which the National Film School had. I think it has less now. Barney was lucky in that all the equipment was available to him and so he could just go out and shoot. He's suffering the results of that now in that he has to go through the painful process of editing it, but he's taught himself Final Cut Pro[5] and is learning how to structure and tell a story – which is really what documentary is about.

Prior to going to the National, you studied Law at Cardiff University and Political Science at Essex University. How have these disciplines impacted upon your career?

Law is the thing that separates civilization from anarchy, so it's probably the most important concept that we live with. You only have to look around you now to see how the rule of law and the belief in law has broken down internationally. The notion of justice has always been a very important one to me. I never really thought that reasonableness was a particularly essential notion, but I have increasingly thought so as I've grown older. Justice and reasonableness are so universal and, if applied correctly, should transcend religion and all the fundamentalisms that currently seem to be screwing us up so much at the moment.

I had a wonderful law teacher called Freddie Farman, who was a bit of prankster and a bit of a ladies' man who drove an Aston Martin and would always start our tutorials with a glass of whiskey. He just had a great deal of style. However, when we got down to the work, he was very erudite and extremely hard-working. I found Freddie to be a fantastic role model. He did so much with his life; he went out and had a good time but was also very successful and an extremely kind person too. I was very attracted to the idea of Law until I started meeting members of the legal profession. I felt that they were very much of the Oxbridge/Eton crowd and very unappealing. It has changed, I hope, but the way to get on then was to date the judge's daughter, get into the right chambers, and go hunting and shooting on weekends. This was not at all what I wanted to do and I became very disillusioned, so I decided to leave Cardiff and go to Essex, which was a politically firebrand university where I had several friends. It was a very happening place in the late sixties.

What also arose from my time at Cardiff – which was then a very working-class town, especially where I lived down in Tiger Bay – was the idea for *Who Cares*. Cardiff has changed a lot; then it was extremely Welsh and I was very much the southerner, but I quite liked being the outsider. Originally I wanted to make *Who Cares* in Tiger Bay, but too much of it was being knocked down. I took a lot of photographs while I was there, especially ones of the burgeoning Muslim community. I liked the diverse mixture of races that existed there. I began to read a lot on the subject, books such as *The People of Ship Street* by Madeline Kerr and *Family and Kinship in East London* by Michael Young and Peter Willmott.

Did other factors lead to your leaving Cardiff?

At the end of my first year in Cardiff I fell in love with an older Norwegian woman whom I had met on a Greek island – the 'Marianne' Leonard Cohen wrote a song about, in fact – and who at this time was living in London. This was very inconvenient for me in my little Morris Minor, which at top speed only reached fifty-five miles an hour. A friend of mine, Kim Longinotto,[6] was at Essex at the time and I soon found myself leaving Cardiff to join her there. I look back upon this now with a certain regret. Essex was much wilder, but also very middle-class.

Was Who Cares *made whilst you were still at Essex, prior to film school?*

It was. In fact, I borrowed the camera from Cardiff. The rugby club had a camera to film their matches, though they never did. It was a pretty good camera. The good thing about Essex University was that they were very open to ideas and they told me that if I made a film then it could count as a year's paper. There had been a really interesting project in the Fuego Islands where the lives of the people who had left the island were filmed and then shown to the people who had remained, and it actually had the effect of reversing the depopulation. So, as a result of this and all the fantastic people I had met in Tiger Bay, I went off and shot *Who Cares*.

How did Liverpool become the eventual location of the film?

Pete Archard, whom I did the film with, was doing a PhD at Liverpool. It was his idea to film there. When I went back, Tiger Bay was simply too far gone. A lot of the streets had been boarded up and it was very difficult to find a street where there was still a tremendous sense of community spirit and also a real mixture of cultures and races.

Community spirit is perhaps the dominant subject of Who Cares. *You capture the tangible camaraderie amongst the people you film, encapsulated best perhaps by the old woman who speaks of the daily ritual of the wives taking it in turns to make tea for everyone. Today the film seems very melancholic.*

When I was making it I had an incredibly strong sense of nostalgia, that modernity has destroyed so much of people's sense of community and placement. Our society has become incredibly mobile and fractured.

Liverpool 8, *Who Cares*

It has become very individualistic; the nuclear family has taken over from those communities where the extended family was still the thing: everybody from street to street knew each other, houses were handed down from generation to generation.

How long did you shoot for?
For about three months.

And did you live amongst the community or did you go backwards and forwards between London and Liverpool?
I lived in Liverpool. Pete Archard had also been in Essex, but I first met him when I was a lifeguard in Cornwall. I am one of the world's worst swimmers and was myself rescued on my third day there. Pete is a very fine academic and was very much an anthropologist who believed in social observation and living amongst the people to understand the particular subculture you are studying. He was very much a part of helping that film happen. He knew Ethel Singleton, that amazing woman at the beginning of *Behind the Rent Strike*; he introduced

13

me to the Singletons, who at that time were living in Liverpool 8 in a really smashed-up house at a place called Myrtle Gardens. Ethel had a very big influence on my political awareness and development, and in a sense *Who Cares* came out of that relationship, as did *Behind the Rent Strike*.7

When I started with *Who Cares*, I really hoped that my films were going to change things. *Who Cares* actually was used as part of a commission on housing but, in a sense, I hoped that I was going to stop slum clearance and that, instead of them destroying the communities, they would actually find a way of preserving the houses and keeping these places intact. I was hoping for changes that were unrealistic. Fred Wiseman said that after the first film he made, he expected the traffic to stop. Of course, it was still all moving, and if he wasn't careful then he was going to get knocked down in the street. It's a bit disillusioning to make something that you are incredibly passionate about and then nothing really happens. You learn to make things that are more targeted. *Who Cares*, for example, is not a very targeted film. Whereas something like *Juvenile Liaison* was very specific and hit the bull's eye. Unfortunately, in doing so it got itself banned – but that's also an indication of its success.

Do you still see this as a role of the documentary? To instigate social change? I ask because your films have a very clear sociological bent. Some claim that it is clearer in your earlier works,8 but one could say it's equally present in the later ones too.
I think that films do make a difference. If you get enough of an audience then you can make a difference. I think that with my two Aileen Wuornos films, people's perceptions of American justice were really altered. You are talking about an audience of many millions – which is not small – and if you add together all the other people who will eventually see the more recent Aileen film, then you can really have an impact. The next time people hear about a serial killer, they will think about what the back story is or wonder what was going on and, I hope, also ask questions about how people who clearly have mental problems should be treated and what our obligations are as a society in our treatment of these people. These are really fundamental questions, and they make the enterprise of making the films, and all the shit that you have to go through, really worthwhile.

It must at least have been gratifying to you that Who Cares *was used as evidence during the Royal Housing Commission?*
Not as much as it should have been, because I don't feel that anything really came of it. I was very passionate about this, and I still really care. It's terrible that we have lost so much of what was really wonderful about these communities. Above all, these communities had people who really cared about each other.

It disheartens me to see towns becoming so homogenized, with independent companies being replaced by conglomerates. Markets are disappearing and most people now shop at one of the large supermarket chains. You see it happening even more on a global scale because capitalism has become entirely global. In material terms, most people today are arguably better off, but I think there was a real sense of extended family and a real brotherhood that we simply don't have any more. Material things can be important, but this sense of brotherhood is one of the fundamentals of life and part of the real fun of it. These people really knew how to have a good time on a Saturday night and that's one of the reasons I really enjoyed being in Liverpool so much. Probably why the film took so long to complete, too . . .

Who Cares *also looks at the result of the influx of West Indians into the community, and there's a great moment where you use the old reggae track 'Feel Like Jumping'.*
The communities were pretty mixed. Liverpool 8, part of an itinerant sea-faring city, had a long tradition of sailors from differing backgrounds and nationalities coming to the area and raising children; it was a real melting pot. There were also some real local characters, such as Johnny Fatso, who claimed to know Eva Peron, and Willie, who swore blind that he was David Bowie's bodyguard. I met all these incredible and diverse people, and I sometimes wish that I could have made a film about each of them. The people were very accepting of each other because they had grown up in an organic and partly irrational way; and what slum clearance and the relocation of people to places like Kirkby did was to split people and communities asunder. All the white people were moved out, whereas the black community was left behind – and I'm convinced that this policy directly led to the later riots in the area. Liverpool 8 became the black ghetto, something it had never been before. Even the last time I went back, the pubs which had previously been very mixed were now predominantly black, which invariably creates a tension.

The interaction between cultures strikes me as a motif of your work.
I find that the British lack of acceptance of outsiders is our most unappealing characteristic. London is now a very cosmopolitan place and is much more interesting for it, but the London I grew up in during the sixties, seventies and early eighties was a very dour and sad kind of place; it felt very isolated from Europe and America and was, I think, very small-minded. This subject is something that I felt very strongly about, especially having experienced the far more liberal atmosphere of sea-faring cities such as Cardiff and Liverpool.

Despite being your first film, Who Cares *is beautifully shot.*
Well, I'd had some experience in stills photography and knew how to work an exposure meter and that kind of thing, and generally I cared very much about composition. In fact, on *Who Cares* I spent more time on composition than I have on any subsequent film. I wasn't using sync sound, and it liberated the image. When you're filming an interview, the sound leads the image because you're restricted to having to film the person talking or the reaction to them talking. This requires a very different kind of technical ability. The way I shot images on *Who Cares* was very specific because the image is the dominant thing. On my subsequent films the image has become subservient to the sound.

Was the decision to shoot in black and white an aesthetic or practical one?
At this time many people were switching from black and white to colour, so people had lots of black-and-white short ends left over.

It suits the material, though. It looks like a film that could have been shot in the thirties.
Who Cares also allowed me to meet Sir Arthur Elton,[9] who got me the money to go and edit it. In this regard the film served as a very good introduction to the business. And Sir Arthur, who was a very charming man, always said that it was like an updated version of *Housing Problems* (1935).[10]

You also credit the novelist Bernice Rubens on Who Cares.
I'd shot all this footage without a clue as to what I was really doing. Then I came back to London, and I remember viewing the film with

my father, who didn't have much of a clue either, and another guy called Steve Peet. And the general feeling was one of 'What on earth is this about?' It was a bit dispiriting. It was also difficult to edit so many hours of material down to eighteen minutes because it was all shot on short ends and was in hundreds of bits. Eventually, I managed to borrow an editing room from a documentary producer named Derek Knight to try and sort through the footage. I was there from seven or eight at night until the cleaner came in early in the morning; after a few months I had chopped up the whole film and hung it, leaving me unable to find a single shot. I had no idea what the story was and at one point, thoroughly exasperated, I dived into the trim bin and began to tear the film up. I knew Bernice Rubens through her two daughters, and she saw what I was going through and told me that I needed to keep things simpler and be more organized. She asked if she could hear the sound tapes and, after listening to them, she more or less wrote a script out. Bernice advised me to do a structure and even suggested what audio should accompany what image. I had also shot lots of material in Greek Orthodox churches and Bernice advised me to cut this out completely, quite rightly, explaining that all this footage belonged in an entirely different film. Bernice saved my bacon.

Who Cares was a real voyage of discovery and an initiation by fire. It's quite pathetic, really, when you consider that it took me almost a year and a half to cut an eighteen-minute film. My son takes great hope from this. The fact that I didn't have synchronized sound actually made it much harder to cut. The rhythm of the film becomes much harder to maintain than if you simply have somebody talking for prolonged periods of time. I'm still quite pleased I took the approach I did, but doing it was absolute agony.

Where was Who Cares *initially shown?*
It had its opening at The OTHER Cinema, where it was presented by Nick Hart-Williams with Gillo Pontecorvo's *The Battle of Algier*s (1965). The NFT also showed it. I personally took it to a few cinemas throughout the country and even did an agit-prop screening in Liverpool in some of the big tenement blocks. I tried to get the old lady whose voice-over I used to come and see it, but she had been rehoused by then and was so unhappy in her new modern home that she just wanted to die; it was terribly sad. In fact, it was dispiriting going back to the old area because most of it had been torn down and all the people

I had met had been rehoused. It was very painful. *Behind the Rent Strike* very much arose through what I saw when I went back and my dismay at how unhappy the community had become; their life force had been cut off. I'll never forget going round to see the woman who had spoken about the communal tea-making. First of all, she wouldn't open her door. Then when she did, the door was on a security chain and it took a long while for her to remember who I was. She looked as if she had aged about a hundred years and in her face was a fear that she hadn't had before. In the old neighbourhood she had been protected from the miscreant youths but now, although she was in a nicer house with her own bath, there were no neighbours around to protect her any more and she was completely on her own. It was really tragic as it was her heart and soul that had made *Who Cares*. There's always a certain amount of pain in making these films, but at the same time I suppose that's what it's all about.

And was it around this time that you decided to go to the National Film School?
Derek Malcolm saw *Who Cares* and wrote an article about it. And, knowing that the National Film School was about to start that year, he arranged a lunch with myself and Colin Young. Colin is a very decep-

Professor Colin Young, Head of
The National Film School

tive character. He looks like a professor with a long straggly beard and he talks in anecdotes, some of which are quite long; you really have to stay with them, because when you get to the end you realize that they're genius. So I kind of got to know Colin before starting at the film school, having generally aimed to arrive at his place just in time for dinner, as he always had really interesting people there. I joined the film school mainly because of Colin. I admired his passion for films; he introduced me to a lot of the *cinema vérité* films that were happening at that time. His big passion was social anthropology and, consequently, observational films that were shot in a particular style. I got to know Richard Leacock, D. A. Pennebaker, Frederick Wiseman, John Marshall, Robert Drew, Jean Rouche and all those film-makers, the founding fathers of the *cinema vérité* movement. The one who really transfixed me right from the beginning was Fred Wiseman. I thought that films such as *Hospital* (1970), *Basic Training* (1971) and *Titicut Follies* (1967) were absolute genius. I still think that they are, and I believe that Wiseman will be the true historian of our times. It's important that his films are also very entertaining and I loved the way that they were shot. I must also say that I adored Wiseman when I finally met him. He's very sophisticated, funny and irreverent, and has a lot to contribute, in a very unpretentious way.

Were there also fiction film-makers whose work attracted your attention?
Well, I liked *Battle of Algiers* (1965), the work of Ken Loach and – no doubt due to the influence of my mother – a lot of the Czech new wave, films such as Jirí Menzel's *Closely Observed Trains* (1966).

Did you become more of a cinephile?
I suppose. The thing with the National Film School was that there weren't any classes as such. People would either come down and show their films or you met them around the dinner table, but there weren't really structured studies; it was very much on an individual basis. I think that *Behind the Rent Strike* and *Proud to Be British* – which I made whilst at the National Film School – were both political statements from a particular position; they weren't really observational films. I certainly learned a lot while I was shooting them and developed the confidence to approach the shooting of them in a much more complicated way. In terms of influence, because they were political

statements they were probably more influenced by my political science and law background as opposed to any particular film or film-maker.

Was it at the film school that you met Joan Churchill?
I met Joan in my last year after she had come there to teach. She had been a student of Colin's at UCLA in California, where he had been a professor. She came over with a friend of hers, Lynzee Klingman, who was a brilliant editor and had cut films like *One Flew Over the Cuckoo's Nest* (1975) for Milos Forman, and they were an amazing duo. That was another notable thing about the National Film School: it was full of these young, amazing people at the top of their profession. Colin was so charismatic that people would drive out to Beaconsfield because they knew that they were going to have a good time.

So Joan came over as this very glamorous figure, and I remember meeting her in Colin's drawing room and finding it very exciting. I took her up to Liverpool, and she and Ethel Singleton got on extremely well. Joan was the first person I met whom I really thought of as a partner that I could work with. The National Film School was very much set up to achieve that; Colin Young's position was that many of the observational ethnographic films he admired were made by partners of two, with one on sound and the other on camera. It's also important to keep personnel to a minimum so as not to appear greater than the subject you're interviewing.

Did Joan and yourself share similar interests and desires in regard to the kinds of films that you wanted to make?
In a sense, we came from similar backgrounds, even though Joan had grown up in America and I had grown up in England. Joan has a fantastic interest in people and is a natural nomad, fantastic at living out of suitcases and up for everything. Some people have this aura about them when you are with them, rather like the Robert Duvall character in *Apocalypse Now* (1979)[11] – you stand next to him and you know that you're never going to get shot. If you go into a film with Joan, you know that you are going to come out the other side; she's like a rock to work with, whereas I can be a bit more giddy. She's very pragmatic too and a great technician, which I'm not – I'm hopeless.

At what stage did the relationship with Joan become personal as well as professional?

Joan Churchill

© Alan Barker

21

This was especially upsetting given how supportive she had been on *Who Cares* and being obviously somebody I looked up to. But I always felt that documentary was about understanding an ideology, without necessarily supporting it. I think my position on that film is very clear, but to someone like Bernice, who's a very pure and a very passionate person, it was too cynical. *Who Cares* was about getting inside and understanding those communities and what they gave to each other; *Proud to Be British* was examining what had enabled this ideology to continue and what kinds of values had been instilled in these people. Ronald Bell himself came from a slightly working-class background and used to take the tube out to the foxhunt. I think that the film covers a tremendously important subject: the need to belong and to acknowledge your betters. And I think that this subject is still very much with us here in Britain.

The film also examines the place of women in society and the behaviour they are expected to exhibit within society, a subject to which you would frequently return.
My girlfriend, the one who later tried to run me over, went to the Oakdene School in Beaconsfield, where I filmed. She was an incredible woman and, even though she was very intelligent and extremely beautiful, she was just expected to marry someone wealthy and not have a career of her own. In fact, she did go on to have a career of her own and has been very successful in it. It's an enormous battle for women who've been brought up in this way to then do something different, to break out of it.

Proud to Be British *also hints at the thinly veiled racism within the school.*
I think that it gives evidence of a lack of information within this country about who these people are. Nowadays people have very little awareness about the fact that these illegal immigrants who everyone keeps harping on about are actually subsidising our supermarkets and doing all the shit jobs that no English people will do – and for meagre salaries each week. The government doesn't want to do anything about it because then all the prices in the supermarkets will have to go up. These people are not eligible for all the basic working benefits that were fought for by the labour movement, and it's a shocking extension of the belief that we were so benevolent and so kind to make their

countries better when we had an empire, and now they want to come over and bleed us dry. Of course, this couldn't be further from the truth. But this attitude is so deeply rooted in our culture.

Film can be so incredibly important because some people just don't know the full extent of what is happening. And then something like the Morecambe Bay[13] incident happens to remind us. What is shocking to me is that there has actually been very little follow-up on the incident; very few people realize that there are these enormous work camps throughout the country that are run by Mafia-style gang-masters who are employing people in appalling conditions in order to enable us to live in the manner to which we are accustomed. This is very simply a twenty-first-century form of slavery. This is something that film can do, and sometimes it is best to tackle these subjects in an accessible or vaguely amusing way because otherwise it is so tragic that you can't deal with it.

The interviewer on the film is credited as Ben Lewin, but I'm sure the voice we hear is yours.
It was a film-school exercise: I shot Ben's film and Ben worked on my film as the interviewer, and I think we both did some of the interviews. I certainly interviewed the guy on the foxhunt, and I remember Derek Malcolm seeing it and telling me that I should never do any more interviews because I sounded like an upper-class git who had been to Eton. This was a bit rich because Derek Malcolm actually *had* been to Eton. I do remember having a real conflict over his comments and thinking that I should get Ben, an Australian, to do the rest of the interviews. I momentarily became rather ashamed of my voice. In fact, I think Derek, who is a lovely, very sweet guy, actually put his comments in print and it took a few years before I thought, 'Fuck it, I am who I am and I'm just going to get on with it.' There was no point my hiding it, so I just made it a creative part of the films.

There's an interesting moment where a policeman stops you from filming and you decide to leave this in the film. This registers that documentary is not entirely objective and that there are film-makers involved in the process.
Absolutely. There were a couple of other similar moments that actually got cut out. I remember that I was filming an exchange between two schoolteachers and one of the teachers being filmed makes a gesture to

stop me filming. My editing tutor told me to cut it out, but I remember Colin Young, who is incredibly post-modern, really regretted that that moment had gone. Colin was really a big one for recognizing the process; he always made the point that, with audiences becoming increasingly sophisticated, it created within them a desire to want to be involved in the process of making the film. I remember him showing a film by an Irish film-maker called Mark McCarty in which an old man being interviewed falls off his bicycle and into a ditch, and McCarty has the choice of putting the camera down and helping or carrying on filming. He puts the camera down on the ground but keeps the camera running and you see the boots of McCarty trudging into the ditch to help this guy out. It's a seminal moment in film-making. It's a very enriching moment that teaches you a lot about McCarty and his relationship to his subject.[14] Colin encouraged you to recognize your own relationship to the subject in the films, and it was very much out of this that I later wanted my relationship with Ethel Singleton to be the introduction to *Behind the Rent Strike*.

This partly touches on the myth of the documentary film-maker objectively capturing some kind of essential truth ...
Real truth is a subjective thing, and films are a subjective statement. They have to be. I always admired a comment by Fred Wiseman when this debate was raging in the eighties and you had people like Roger Graef rather pretentiously saying that his *The Space Between the Words* series was closer to the truth than anybody else's work. Wiseman replied that his films were 'reality fiction', in that he filmed them as reality, but by the time that he had edited them they had become a work of fiction. I think that Fred is much closer to the reality of the situation.

Behind the Rent Strike *was Broomfield's graduation film at the National Film School. Divided into two sections ('The Social Conditions' and 'The Political Reaction'), it examines the action taken in 1973 by the residents of Kirkby New Town in Liverpool in response to the Housing Finance Bill and their unacceptable living conditions. As well as simply but effectively documenting the strike itself, Broomfield also unobtrusively films inside Ruffwood Comprehensive School and a poultry factory staffed entirely by female workers, thus presenting the restrictive educational and occupational avenues with which the residents of the community are faced.*

You frequently do follow-up pieces and invariably maintain contact with the leading figures in your work, such as Voletta Wallace from Biggie and Tupac.

That's true. To be fair, I haven't spoken to Ethel Singleton for a couple of years, but I've known her since 1969 and have a real love for her and her family.

Did Behind the Rent Strike *arise directly from the making of* Who Cares?

The thing that got me to go back there was my relationship with Ethel Singleton and her family, whom I'd stayed in touch with after doing *Who Cares* and had gone to visit a few times. I also wanted *Proud to Be British* and *Behind the Rent Strike* to be viewed together; to present two sides of the coin. By this time I was making films with sync sound and I suppose I felt that my relationship with Ethel should be very much a part of what the film should be about – so, in a sense, this was

Mother and child, *Behind the Rent Strike*

the first film that I put myself in as a character. You don't see me, but the intention was very much what later became my style.

The fiercely intelligent and politicised
Ethel Singleton, *Behind the Rent Strike*

It seems that it is Ethel who drags you into it. You are asking her questions but she turns the tables and begins to ask you to express your views about why you are making the film.
I think this is really where it came from. We had a very inspirational relationship, certainly for me anyway. Ethel schooled me and educated me politically about the differences between the life that I had had and the reality of a lot of other people's lives. She was articulate and wise enough to be able to do it, as well as being very realistic about my role as a filmmaker and what I could and couldn't achieve with my work.

Behind the Rent Strike was made in a very political time; it was a time when I was trying to work out my own political beliefs and feelings, and I was, in a sense, coming to Ethel for her opinions and for her take on life. I would endlessly engage her in conversation and frequently quite heated arguments and discussions long into the night. She was very kind and generous towards me, but at the same time had no illusions as to who I was.

Perhaps a film that was simply conversations would have made a better film than *Behind the Rent Strike*. I don't know. Again, I was doing a more political analysis kind of thing, but Ethel was originally the touchstone for that.

In the film, she takes you to task for being a middle-class film-maker making a film about the working classes.
Ethel is undoubtedly my best friend from the area and, when I made that film, I was actually staying in her house with her husband Jim and her four children. In the evenings Ethel would sit in the chair that you see in the film, and we would have these very intense discussions and arguments, just as in the film. There was a great fondness between us, and a lot of it was her informing me about the fact that there was a very different world and a very different way of seeing the world than the way in which I'd been brought up.

Did you feel a sense of naivety?
Of course I did. That was partly why I was there. I thought that the only way I was going to learn anything – and this goes for all the films that I've made – was by finding out first-hand about them. For me, rather than reading, the best way to learn is by going out and pounding the pavements, making the relationships and finding out first-hand what is really going on. Ethel was extremely articulate and believed in me enough to find the time to have discussions. I honestly believe that if she had grown up in a slightly different class and at a different time, then she would have been a great political leader, because she was also an amazing orator. I have seen Ethel stand up in front of a crowd of several thousand people and really move them to tears. She speaks from the heart, but at the same time she has an amazing social awareness. Ethel has had a tough life but she's a really big person; it was phenomenal meeting someone like that.

Ethel initially seemed very wary of the likely effect of Behind the Rent Strike, *stating that the film will make no difference and then you will return to your middle-class life.*
Her comments are quite true. One of the contradictions of making these films is that you always go back to your own life. In fact, if you didn't, you would go nuts.

The film is structured in two parts. Was that always your intention or did you merely react to the environment in which you were filming?
It wasn't always my intention, but it did fall into that. The structure of the film is frankly a bit of a mess, in that you have Ethel, who wasn't living in the middle of Kirkby but in a place called Queen's Drive, but who was still involved with the rent strike, offering comment on the social conditions. The majority of the other people I filmed – such as the family at the beginning of the film, the victims of the social conditions Ethel is describing – did live in Kirkby.

Like Ethel, the family are extremely articulate.
They were. The father of the family was a very sweet and passionate guy. The tragedy of that situation was that the woman had become addicted to tranquillizers and had tried to take her own life. I had no real relationship with these people, but I found their situation absolutely shocking. In a way it hardens you when you hear these awful things because it is so overwhelming and totally unfair. You very much feel that if you inform people in other parts of the country that this is what is happening and that these aren't just a bunch of layabouts who just can't be fucked to pay the rent, but that their conditions are appalling and that their whole life-horizons are totally different from the ones we know, then maybe there will be a shifting of positions. The other distressing thing was the proximity of the playing fields, on which the children couldn't play. I think that is one of the most incredible images in the film. I actually shot that image myself and I feel that it works very well.

Around the time of the making of *Behind the Rent Strike* I became very interested in issues concerning housing and community. These have always been very close to my heart – alongside architecture and the questions of the living environments you create for people, and how people also build for themselves. Perhaps people should build for themselves, because whilst doing research in Paris I met a number of architects who had built accommodation for working-class people and – though many of them were well meaning and had social issues close to their heart – the fact was that they didn't really respect the organic way communities develop and what was already there. I always thought that architecture was about building from what *is* as opposed to a more conceptual approach. The people of *Behind the Rent Strike* would have been so much happier if, rather than being moved to new buildings and new areas, the architects had simply modernized one side of their street and then the other. I may be being naive, but they should have left the people where they were. There was also an inhumanity to the conditions in which the people of Kirby had to work; the factories – now long gone – were appalling, and there was no facilitation of a social life. There were no cinemas or dance halls; these had all gone. All the young people were in the middle of nowhere and completely cut off because it was too expensive for them to get into town.

You film inside one of these factories when you show some female workers doing what looks like the most repellent of tasks.
That's right. They are pulling the carcasses of chickens apart to make chicken pies. What an awful job.

It's very skilfully edited, though, because the soundtrack is of another female describing an idyllic holiday spent busking in Ireland. It's a very poignant moment. Was it at this time that you began to realize the tremendous potential of the documentary medium to dramatically make such points and connections?
I think so. Godard's *British Sounds* (1969) has one great tracking shot that I really admired. There was also a moment from *The Hour of the Furnaces* (1968) when some kids run alongside a train – this reminded me of the kids running alongside the cars in Kirkby. The tragedy is that it's not as if these people can't appreciate beauty and happiness; it's not as if they're not poets.

Behind the Rent Strike *also has a very funny juxtaposition of the Gideon Bible representatives handing out bibles at a local school that you follow with a very funny, Kes-like lecture from a visiting policeman who slowly rounds on the kids and bullies and cajoles them into accepting that they have no future.*

31

Factory workers preparing chicken carcasses for pies,
Behind the Rent Strike

It was out of this scene that *Juvenile Liaison* came. The point of the school scene, and then the factory scene, was to act as an illustration of what was expected of the children in Kirkby. They weren't expected to go to university; in fact, they weren't expected to do very much. I felt that the whole attitude of the policeman and the bible people was indicative of that. These people were expected to be submissive, so the police treated them like that. Their brushes with the law were generally very abrasive and the policeman's whole attitude was patronizing and condescending. There was also a complete lack of respect – something that runs through most of British education. I think that the schools there were somewhat up against it, but there didn't seem much attempt to invigorate the children into pursuing something that would interest them; they seemed more concerned with knocking them down.

A visiting policeman puts the fear of
god into pupils at a local school

Was the policeman happy to be filmed?
He was fine about it and through him I got hold of the juvenile-liaison
people and then went ahead and did the *Juvenile Liaison* film. In both
cases I was very interested in the way in which the police dealt with the
working classes. Many of the people they were dealing with come
from very socially deprived backgrounds, who clearly should be dealt
with by social services. But the police end up dealing with them, even
though they're clearly not trained to. They aren't social workers; they
have been trained in the very gruff manner of interrogation.

*Did the attitudes of the teachers and the authority figures also strike a
chord in relation to your own experiences at school?*
They certainly rekindled a lot of my own feelings about school, which
was how irrelevant most of it was and how out-of-step it was with
what most of the kids were actually thinking about. I realized that

there was a very prescribed way of teaching that really had nothing to do with the experiences of the people who had grown up in Kirkby or of the reality that was there. It's a joke trying to get those people interested in the Gideon Bible; and the police officer similarly wasn't adding anything.

That film was shown on television, and one of the teachers who we see disciplining a young child who had been involved in a fight with another child then got into terrible trouble. There was an inquiry within the school, and I was asked to come back and talk about what had happened and the actions of the teacher. I remember commenting that I didn't think that the teacher had done anything unusual; he'd just had the misfortune of being filmed. The way that the teacher behaved was something I had seen time and time again, and rather than victimizing this individual the authority in question would have done better to look at the way that their teachers were collectively behaving towards their pupils. I have found this with my work repeatedly: the institutions take it out on the individual whom you show in the film, rather than actually looking at themselves and wondering whether their whole approach isn't wrong.

Your being called back to 'give evidence' is a pattern that recurs throughout your work, a more recent example being Aileen: The Life and Death of a Serial Killer, *where you are summoned to what becomes a character assassination of her lawyer, Steve Glazer.*
And quite rightly, I feel, in that instance. It was foolhardy and stupid but also an indictment of a system that would enable someone with no experience to take on a capital case. You would never be allowed to do that in this country. There are other examples where my work has been used in this way – *Tattooed Tears* and *Soldier Girls*, for example. Following *Juvenile Liaison*, Sergeant Ray had an enormous shadow cast over the rest of his career and had a dreadful time in Blackburn after the film came out. The drill sergeant in *Soldier Girls* had the same thing happen, and in both instances I felt terrible. It's a consequence of these kinds of films and, in a way, I stopped doing that particular type of documentary because it is not pleasant to have to shoulder the burden of responsibility for fucking up someone's career and life. I felt particularly strongly for Sergeant Ray, who was a well-meaning and very nice man who was also a family guy and a very respected member of the community. I genuinely think that my film contributed to destroying his life.

34

I was interested by the sequence in Behind the Rent Strike *where you show a news crew reporting from outside the Tower Hill estate. Why was this shot important to you?*
I felt that the media got it so wrong. This is how news reports are done and these are the news reports you see every day on television. And they are stupid and generally don't get anywhere near close enough to the situation they are reporting on. It's a very glib report. There's this notion within the media that a professional broadcaster does things in a particular way, that they should look a particular way and should always appear in control. The reality is that they are rarely in control in situations that are inherently out of control.

How strong was the sense of solidarity in an environment where people were choosing to go to prison in response to escalating rent prices and degenerating living conditions?
The rent strike had the effect of bringing people closer together. For example, all the housewives would meet up and throughout the process they became much more politicized. Some of the husbands resented this because, in some cases, their spouses were way ahead of them in their understanding of the political ramifications of the rent strike and its wider significance.

How difficult was it to film the final sequences of the film, with the crowded strikers outside the courts and the heavy police presence?
Funnily enough, they weren't that difficult to film because there were so few people filming in this way and there was a great respect for it amongst both the police and the demonstrators. What was quite amusing was that when we turned the camera on and got close to the crowd, everyone would start rioting and pushing the police around. When we were reloading, this would all stop, so there was an aspect of their playing up for the purposes of the camera. I also think that a lot of the police were actually on the side of the demonstrators as they came from similar backgrounds and knew what their actions were about. Liverpool is, of course, a very naturally political area so it was liberating for me to work up there. A lot of the time I was working alone with somebody called Philip Jones Griffiths, who was running Magnum, the photographic agency. Philip was also somebody who had been to Vietnam and had produced a magnificent book titled *Vietnam Inc.* During the filming Philip's mother was dying in Wales, so we would often meet in the morn-

ing and then Philip would have to travel to Wales, leaving me alone. I had to carry all the filming equipment around in a big pram because it was so bleeding heavy – it enabled me to become very close to the people up there and I really loved them.

It was a very difficult film, initially, because there were all these militant political groups up there who were vying for the favours of the rent strike and, at first, I was regarded as just a public-school twit; but I was very determined that I was not going to apologize for who I was. There was a bit of an initiation by fire, but I got to know the people well by staying up there for so long and sleeping on the floors of the people I had met. In fact, when they raided the cash-and-carry I think it was the National Film School Land Rover I was driving that was used to load up.

Do you think that people who know your work only from the more recent films would be surprised by the earlier ones?
I think they probably would be. Especially with something like *Kurt and Courtney* – though maybe less so than with the *Aileen* films, which go back to the essence of my work. I was very angry at the time that I made *Kurt and Courtney* and very sick of celebrity in America, and I just wanted to put my bazooka up it and cause as much damage as I could. *Biggie and Tupac* is a more responsible piece of work that could perhaps have been more pointed but was certainly a way out of all that stuff. *Aileen: The Life and Death of a Serial Killer* was very much back to my roots and why I did what I did as a documentary film-maker.

In terms of the times that we live in, there is a certain resurgence in political interest and Bush's greatest present to all of us is that he has made us political again. He has gone so far that people have realized that they have to do something because they were drowning in a sea of consumerism and were losing touch with the bigger picture. This is his contribution to our lives and I think that this is reflected in my work. *Heidi Fleiss: Hollywood Madam* is one of my favourite films because I felt that it was political with a small 'p', but political nonetheless: political about the lives and relationships of people in a place like Los Angeles and, for me, very accurate. *Kurt and Courtney* is really to do with celebrity, and there was a time when I was in America when I wanted the films to be more commercial. It has always been a battle as a documentary film-maker and a battle that I have personally fought for a long time to make films that are worth making that are also commercially successful. Now we have entered a phase where documentaries are much more commercial enterprises.

Another relatively recent change is that documentaries are now largely being produced for the cinemas as opposed to being produced purely for television.
I was actually one of the few documentary makers in the seventies and eighties who was making documentaries that would be theatrical features. *Juvenile Liaison* was intended to be a theatrical feature in 1976, and *Soldier Girls* played extensively in cinemas in the US. This was very unusual and difficult, and it's wonderful that this is finally being recognized.

There's a very fertile climate now for documentary.
There is, and I think that's so fantastic. The success of Michael Moore's films and titles such as *When We Were Kings* (1996),[15] *Hoop Dreams* (1994),[16] *Kurt and Courtney* (which did well theatrically both here and in the US) and Kevin Macdonald's *Touching the Void* (2003) really opened up the doors. Previously you were lucky to break even theatrically.

Has commercial viability led to a dilution in terms of the subject matters covered?
No, I don't think so. I think that if they are going out theatrically, they have to be more detailed and more studied and separate themselves from being just a television programme. Going the extra thirty or forty minutes from the standard sixty-minute TV programme is very difficult. It's not just those extra minutes, it's being substantially different in the whole presentation and depth and scope of the subject. I also think that a lot of the recent documentaries we have seen are of a very high technical standard.

We also seem to have entered a more sophisticated moment and moved away from the very simplistic talking-head format. Though, having said that, one of the most fascinating documentaries of the last couple of years is Hitler's Secretary *(2002).*
André Heller, who appears in *Driving Me Crazy*, was the co-director of that film.[17] I've yet to see it, but it sounds very similar to *The*

Confessions of Winifred Wagner (1975) by Hans-Jürgen Syberberg. This film – and, it sounds to me, André's film – was very much a stylistic decision. With the Winifred Wagner film, the camera zooms back for ten minutes and then zooms forward for ten minutes so that you just look at this woman and have history envelop your mind; it's almost like someone doing a monologue. But I think that it is still a theatrical film. The mess occurs when people don't know their style and haven't really decided which story they are telling. A lot of television documentaries don't work because they are a mish-mash of styles and subjects.

Do you think form and style should be subservient to content?
I think that the question of structure is more important. Quite frequently, documentary films don't work because there are inconsistencies within the rules of the framework that the film has established for itself; that was the thing that Colin Young was particularly good on. He was really good on structure, partly because he had studied form and logic at university and had then worked for military intelligence; he had an incredible mind when it came to working out what the form and what the structure is. I suppose this is what film-making is all about: it's about storytelling, it's about the form you take to tell the story. Andrew Jarecki's *Capturing the Friedmans* (2003) is a wonderful film but there are irritations within it; for example, you cut back constantly to the mother in the same place, which gives the impression that somebody has gone through and cut the interview up to prove a point, rather than going back to the interview at a different date to move the film on.

Notes
1. Maurice Broomfield's most recent exhibition, 'Photographs', was held at the Elms Lesters Gallery, London WC2, 12–20 March 2004.
2. 'Nick had a lot of problems at school. It wasn't that he was disruptive as such. It was more that he was always reluctant to be taught the correct way of doing things.' Maurice Broomfield, in Xan Brooks, 'Factory Records', *Guardian*, 3 March 2004.
3. 'Nick Broomfield: The Fly in the Ointment', in Pearson, Allison, *Imagining Reality: The Faber Book of Documentary*, p. 345.
4. Known as Church, Robert Churchill founded Churchill Films in LA. One of the most successful educational film companies, it also provided a training school for many subsequently successful Hollywood film-makers.
5. Final Cut Pro is the creative, professional and extensible tool for editing and

finishing in SD and HD formats. The application provides unmatched scalability, precision editing tools and seamless workflow. Upon its introduction it revolutionized the editing process.

6. Kim Longinotto's films include: *Underage* (1982), *Eat the Kimono* (1989), *Divorce Iranian Style* (1998), *Gaea Girls* (2000) and *The Day I Will Never Forget* (2002).

7. This was the film with which Broomfield later graduated from the National Film School.

8. 'After Broomfield and Churchill split up, it became clear that it had been Joan who had the social conscience.' Pearson, *op. cit.*, p. 349.

9. Sir Arthur Elton was part of a group of Cambridge University students – who also included Stuart Legg and Humphrey Jennings – who formed the influential Empire Marketing Board (EMB) film unit. Evolving from the GPO Film Unit, the aim of the EMB was to apply the knowledge acquired in government to service to industry.

10. Produced by the Gas, Light and Coke Company, *Housing Problems* highlights the social problem of poor housing and its solution in the slum-clearance programme and the rebuilding of new homes fitted with gas appliances. Shot in the slums of London, the film features remarkably candid direct-to-camera interviews.

11. Lt. Col. Bill Kilgore.

12. Mike Radford's films include *1984* (1984) and *Il Postino* (1995).

13. On 5 February 2004 twenty-one cocklers drowned as they worked at Hest Bank, near Morecambe. The cocklers, who were caught by the rising tide, were refugee workers from the Fuqing area of south-east China. The incident caused a massive inquest into the abuse of working conditions for foreign workers in the UK.

14. *The Village*, Mark McCarty, 1966.

15. Directed by Leon Gast.

16. Directed by Steve James.

17. Co-directed by André Heller and Othmar Schmiderer, *Blind Spot: Hitler's Secretary* is a frills-free interview with Traudl Junge, one of Hitler's personal secretaries during World War II.

2

Skeletons and Scapegoats

Whittingham, Fort Augustus, Marriage Guidance, Juvenile Liaison, Juvenile Liaison 2

Sargeant Ray and Glen in the police
cell, *Juvenile Liaison*

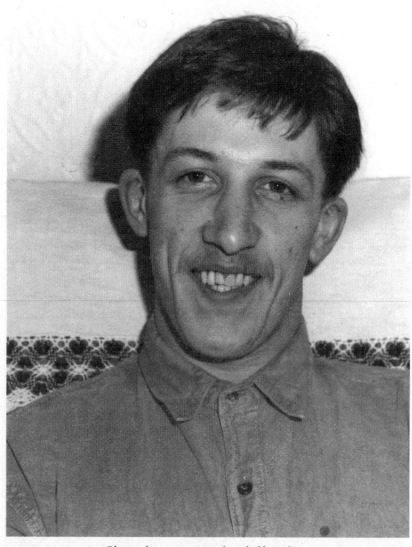
Glen today, a supermarket shelf-stacker,
Juvenile Liaison, 2

NB: I think that we should talk about both *Whittingham* and *Fort Augustus* as, in a sense, they go together. They were both done with Ray Gosling for Granada Television. *Whittingham* was the first one and was shot in a mental hospital in Preston. In a way, that was a Wiseman influence. There were good moments in the film, but it was shot much too quickly. On the strength of *Whittingham*, I was commissioned to shoot *Fort Augustus*, a film about a Benedictine monastery located on the shores of Loch Ness. I went back to Fort Augustus last year and the monastery had been closed down and was up for sale, and most of the monks I had met were now in the cemetery. I think that they originally agreed to the film because they were a dwindling community and they hoped that the film would somehow help them.

I don't think that either of the films are particularly good, but *Fort Augustus* had some interesting moments, especially the ones with Ray Gosling, who was the interviewer, getting stuck when engaging the monks in theological discussions. He was clearly unable to compete with them and so would turn to the camera and say, 'I'm stuck. What should I do next?' and I simply left all this in the film. Granada's reaction was that Ray was a professional interviewer and professional interviewers don't get stuck, so they told me to cut these sequences out. I refused and then the abbot got involved and wrote various letters. I put up a fight, and then Ray pleaded with me to change the film and it all started to get very nasty. The film got recut. I was less than enthusiastic with the new version and never worked with Granada again. It's one of the few times – this was around the same time as *Juvenile Liaison* – where I didn't have the authority or control. I think it shows signs of self-importance to believe that the community may still be alive had the first version of the film gone out, but I think that you assume a real responsibility towards the people who have let you into their lives to make the best possible film you can. With a television schedule of just ten days' shooting, you cannot really do that. You need to be there for a minimum of five weeks to truly become a part of the community and really get in there. In a sense, this is your repayment to the community for entrusting their lives to you. The year 1976, when *Juvenile Liaison* was banned, was a great disappointment to me. It was the year of my exit from the UK.

Because of industry stipulations I had to work with a crew of five or six people on *Whittingham* and *Fort Augustus* – there was just really no way around it, which was partly why I did *Marriage Guidance*.

Another commission, this time for Thames Television, Marriage Guidance *looked at numerous couples undergoing marriage-guidance therapy. The film was shot with Joan Churchill over a six-month period.* On that film I only had two people in the room and the rest of the crew could all just sit outside in the van, running the engine and drinking too much, which, to be honest, is what they did. It was a great situation where I didn't have to have them around and so they couldn't really affect the film. England was not a good place to work then.

Richard and Charmaine, *Marriage Guidance*

44

JW: *So Marriage Guidance was really made because it could be just you and Joan filming in the room?*

In part. But *Marriage Guidance* was potentially a really good film. Had I not done it for television, I would have continued on with it. It was the only one that I made for British television that was semi-commissioned that at the time I felt proud of. I remember that Dennis Potter wrote the most scathing review of it, stating that it was totally voyeuristic and intrusive, but I didn't think so. The film could have gone further than it did. But it started from a really interesting premise.

Broomfield's next undertaking, Juvenile Liaison, *follows the day-to-day activities of a juvenile-liaison unit in Blackburn, Lancashire. Tracking Sergeant Ray and his fellow officers over a three-and-a-half-month period as they deal in a no-nonsense fashion with young offenders from impoverished working-class backgrounds, the film offers a case study both of the work the officers undertake and of the sometimes questionable methods they employ. Subsequently only screened at the House of Commons following objections by the police and the refusal of the British Film Institute to release the film, the experience led to Broomfield and Joan Churchill returning to the area in 1990 to make the follow-up film* Juvenile Liaison 2. *Taken from the perspective of many of the young offenders and their families involved in the first film – and comprised of interviews with a good number of them – the film looks at what has become of many of those who came to the attentions of the juvenile-liaison unit and how attitudes towards the short, sharp shock treatment the police previously employed may have altered. The effects of the original* Juvenile Liaison *film on Sergeant Ray, who was chastised by the police and the community, are also presented.*

We were introduced to Sergeant Ray as being the best juvenile-liaison officer running the best department in that part of Lancashire. There were three officers in total and they were all highly regarded within the community and the police, and we followed them around for a month and a half to a couple of months filming particular cases. The film is really a case study and not so much a structured work in the way that *Soldier Girls* was later on; stylistically it's more like *Tattooed Tears*. For me it was a big departure from what I'd done in that we had enough money to gather together a lot of film. *Behind the Rent Strike* and *Proud to Be British* were very well thought out in terms of the scenes I needed and much more conceptual. This was much more a case of following the action as it unfolded.

Joan and I were both shooting at this time, as neither of us wanted to do sound. This was somewhat tricky, so it was agreed that I would film the first two cases and then we would switch. And we did, but my filming was not very sophisticated. I was a bit of a carthorse and kept a fairly wide frame and allowed people to move around in it whilst I moved around as little and as reluctantly as possible, so as not to give away that I didn't exactly know where the focus was; whereas Joan, who had shot Alan and Susan Raymond's *An American Family* (1973) and was highly gifted, could do a whole operetta of what was going on in the room. When we came to screen the two versions side-by-side, we absolutely couldn't use them because they were two different films and, very grudgingly, I moved over to do the sound recording – which was something that I came to love enormously but at this point resented enormously. It felt like a demotion.

It was just the two of us and we had a whole lot of film magazines, so we could shoot for about an hour, just following the liaison officers around as they did their work dealing with children below the age of criminal responsibility. It was supposed to be a scheme that would keep potential offenders out of court – a 'short, sharp shock' kind of thing – and so there was a certain amount of co-operation between schools, who would haul them in, and parents, who were having problems with kids that they could not control. The officers were policemen who had not received any special training other than their normal police training, and the way in which they dealt with the kids was very much a reflection of that in terms of the way that they questioned the children and the punishments that they thought were appropriate. At the same time, one of our main interests in making the film was that Blackburn was a very run-down cotton town with high unemployment and a lot of problems with truancy. The community was very dependent on the authorities, the social services and the police, and we wanted to capture a part of industrial Britain that had not made any sort of transition.

Was the sense of community spirit that was so apparent in Who Cares *entirely absent here?*

I got no sense of any kind of real community. There was a big Asian population moving in who were extremely resented. The area was very run-down and people were quite uneducated. The houses people lived in were utterly depressing and seemed to be covered in this really garish wallpaper that would send you into hallucinations. I guess that a lot of people had originally worked in the mills, but these had now all closed down. When we went back to make the updated film, *Juvenile Liaison 2*, we found that a lot of the kids were on drugs and some of them obviously had very little time left to live. So that was the setting.

There's a sequence with a young Asian girl who is accused of stealing pencils, and what becomes all too apparent from the reaction of her teachers and from the female police officer who visits the girl's parents is that there is absolutely no understanding of this culture. The police officer is unable even to understand what the father of the girl is saying.

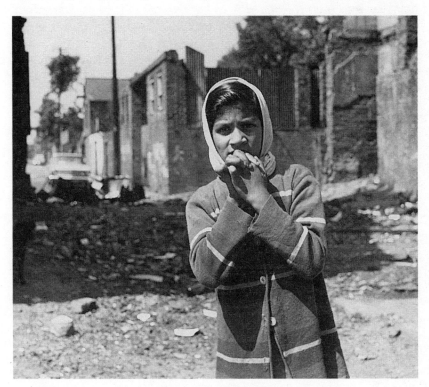

Rashida, *Juvenile Liaison*

I think that this is what has exploded into support for the BNP. The girl in the film, Rashida, was actually a very bright girl who, had she been schooled in the right way, was certainly university material. But maybe culturally it was too much of a leap for those teachers, who had such a prescribed sense of who they were going to be teaching: white kids from a very particular background. One of the troubles, for all of us really, is that we grow up and are taught in a very particular moment of history, but history does not continue in that moment, so somebody who is trained at one moment will be out of date twenty years later – which was certainly the case with these teachers, who certainly needed to be retrained. They weren't necessarily bad people with a sadistic dark side to them; they were largely well-meaning people who just so happened to be a little out of their depth.

In the follow-up we hear that Rashida has married a devout Muslim and that she's been forbidden from speaking to you by her husband.
I remember being very depressed by this because I always felt that Rashida was a real bright spark and certainly had done nothing worse than I had ever done at school. I sort of admired her and found it quite endearing when she tried to take the confiscated pencils back – it was a moment of pure genius. It's tragic that somebody who could have contributed so much to the community is probably forbidden from doing so. You could sense her fate from the attitude of her father, who was such an orthodox man himself; fundamentalism is quite often the need to attain a total identity. I must go back and relook at *Juvenile Liaison* because the making of the film, and particularly the aftermath, was such a painful and emotional process.

The scene from Juvenile Liaison *that caused the most trouble and controversy involves a young child being put in a police cell when he is suspected of stealing a cowboy suit. The moment is very difficult to watch, so one can only imagine how harrowing it must have been to witness and film.*
The truth of it is that we knew we had a fantastic scene that was going to make the film. And you're thinking 'Whoopee!' – but at the same time we both knew that the situation was dreadful and really quite ridiculous. Also, to be absolutely honest, you realize that Sergeant Ray's career is going to be left in shreds when this gets shown. Making a film is a bit like being in a hostage situation: you become good

friends with whomever you are filming because you share so many intimacies over a long period of time. We became very close to Sergeant Ray, so I was probably thinking, 'I know that this is not a bad man. It's unfortunate he's doing this and that I'm filming it. It's going to make a great film but he's going to be screwed . . .' Of course, it's totally inappropriate what he does with that poor little kid, who was probably autistic and comes from a tragic and awful household.

It's probably very different for a viewer who is just with the film for those ninety minutes and hasn't had the two-month relationship with Sergeant Ray that we had. We'd been in his house and knew his family and had spent many hours with him in the police station. So there was a lot of loyalty to him. But an audience seeing the film would most likely only identify with the kid.

There is a strong sense of verbal and physical abuse running through the film – not just from the police but from the families of the children too.

Sargeant Ray gives George a wake-up call,
Juvenile Liaison

49

I can't tell you . . . some of the houses we went into, especially the house where George lives, the one who Sergeant Ray pulls out of bed. Everywhere you looked there was another kid. It was obvious that George was not well, and the humiliation that his family allows him to endure is awful. I also felt that we were guilty of adding to his humiliation by being there. Again, one knew that one was getting a great scene, but there is a real awkwardness to the situation.

All those families were very subservient to the state and were so downtrodden and so unused to speaking their minds because it had been ingrained in them that they had nothing useful to say. The one person who was slightly defiant was Rashida, which was why she was so refreshing – and look what happened to her. That's the reality of it and I wonder if it has changed.

There is one other defiant character: the father of one of the children whom Sergeant Brooks accuses of shoplifting in Woolworth's.
I think that they did doubt authority and its values, and it was very apparent that the police really disliked this family. They had a spirit and defiance to them.

The fact that Sergeant Ray suffered so terribly at the hands of the authorities and was rapidly removed from his post – was that especially upsetting to you personally?
I really felt that we ruined him, and for no good reason, given that the film was buried for thirteen years. It wasn't shown anywhere except to a parliamentary committee in the House of Commons, but there weren't any substantial changes made to the training of juvenile-liaison officers as a result of the film.

It was a very important experience for Joan and I in that it ensured that I demanded copyright on all my subsequent films. The reality of *Juvenile Liaison* was that we spent over a year on it and we then had no rights over the film. We worked our balls off for over a year, earning thirty quid a week, staying in really shitty B&Bs with these awful nylon sheets that we slid around on. And then we didn't even own the film. The film was basically banned, and this made me want to go and work in America for a while, where there weren't such constraints and there was much more a feeling of the public right to know than there was in England at that time.

As well as demanding copyright and a back-end so that I could share in the success of the film if it was successful, I think I was one of the first documentary film-makers to go to meetings with a lawyer. People were amazed and quite indignant. They wouldn't take my lawyer's calls, so I refused to make the film. If they wanted the film enough, they relented. Also, I went along with a load of other film-makers to the BFI to demand to be given back the copyright on my work, and I think that I was the only one who got it.

I notice that you have your own archives here at the house.
If you look at people like Pennebaker and Wiseman, they all have their own archives. Pennebaker is especially fastidious, partly because he still lives off the older titles. Wiseman, in his typical way, just chucked everything into a room in his house, but nonetheless he has done it. Richard Leacock, interestingly, didn't archive his work and hasn't retained it as an entire body. This is a massive shame because he is just as great a talent as the others but because of his lack of archiving he is in danger of not being remembered in the same way. I just saw him in Prague and even he doesn't know where most of it is: a lot of his films have just disappeared – it's tragic. I'm a good friend of Molly Dineen[1] and I keep constantly saying, 'Molly, for God's sake find your masters and all your bits and pieces. Keep them together so that you can get your films out and recirculate them.'

I spend a lot of time between films making sure my website is up to date and that my library, mainly stored in Santa Monica – probably the worst place to store stuff as it is right by the sea – is also maintained. It's run by a wonderful woman called Jo Harkins.

Who originally commissioned Juvenile Liaison?
The British Film Institute gave us a grant. The BFI had given me completion money on *Who Cares* and then they put up £30,000 for us to do *Juvenile Liaison*. Barry Gavin was the head of the production board at the time and he was entirely supportive of the film, resigning from the production board in defence of it. It was a tragedy that the BFI backed down.

They refused to release it?
Yes. The police argument was that they wanted to protect the identity of the kids, but I didn't think that the kids had done anything wrong. It was so transparent that the police were covering up for themselves,

and there would have been an outcry if the film had been released on TV. Thames TV had bought it and loved it and would have created a very interesting debate about what training was appropriate for the police; and, more specifically, a wider debate about what is the correct way to deal with kids. It would have been a great piece of television.

Did the police not also insinuate that you hadn't gained the correct release forms?
Yes, they did; so then we went round all the parents and got other consent forms. I was particularly disappointed with Roger Graef, who was on the board of governors at the BFI, because we had shown him the new release form that we were going to go back to the parents with and he had actually approved it – and then still wouldn't support the film. I feel that the BFI and Keith Lucas, in particular, who was the governor, should be really ashamed of what they did, and so should Roger Graef. Up to that point I had regarded him as a colleague, but I still can't look him in the eye. I don't harbour grudges but I can never respect somebody who behaved in such a weak way. Joan and I felt very embattled and very unsupported. But it did encourage me never again to put myself in such a position as a film-maker. I was certainly angry and I told them all what I thought of them. I tend to react by trying to find ways around such things.

Was Juvenile Liaison 2 *some years later one such way around it?*
Yes, and it was a way of giving the BFI an excuse to release the first one. It was also fascinating going back to Blackburn – we had to actually hire a detective to find out what had happened to a couple of the people. A few of the families had disappeared right off the social radar and were in such poverty that they had become sub-people and weren't on any electoral rolls at all. One of the things that the original film was criticized for was that, because we went in with the police, we didn't really have a separate relationship with the families. In a sense, we were making a film specifically about the police scheme, and the emotional nature of the film was such that many people were really riled by what they had seen happening to these children. People like things to be resolved so that they can leave the screening room without feeling that they need to find somewhere to deposit their emotions. And I found in screening this film that there was a lot of anger – what I felt was misplaced anger. People were very angry that we had not

George today with the Salvation Army,
Juvenile Liaison 2

established a relationship with the families independent of the police and that we didn't have an opportunity to get the families' point of view of what had happened. It's quite true; we didn't have a separate dialogue with the families and, because Sergeant Ray had already come in for a lot of criticism and a police investigation for his handling of the cases, we weren't able to rekindle our relationship with Sergeant Ray when we went back. This was very painful and, as I said before, what institutions tend to do is victimize the individual rather than looking at their training programme in general. The easiest thing to do was to make Sergeant Ray a scapegoat.

So going back to Blackburn was a mixture of things. Some of the children were in a better state but, on the whole, it was an area that was still in a very sad situation.

The first film certainly did terminate Sergeant Ray's career. If someone asked me for the skeletons in my career then Sergeant Ray would be one of the main ones. I again stress that it was all so unnecessary because, as the first film was suppressed, there was never the level of public debate that I had intended, either in terms of questioning police procedure or in terms of the parents in the film looking at how they were treating their children.

So if the first film hadn't been banned and it had led to these debates, would it then have been justifiable to have sacrificed Sergeant Ray?
I would have felt that his career had been sacrificed for a just cause. But also, had there been that debate, then Ray wouldn't have been so easily victimized, because then it would have been a debate on the whole scheme – but that debate never happened so Ray was sacrificed. This could also have been the outcome if the BFI hadn't behaved like a bunch of neutered lambs and had stood up to the police. I remember having a pee in one of the urinals at the National Film Theatre where the meetings between the Lancashire police and the BFI took place, and the assistant chief constable turned to me and said, 'I wouldn't like to have this lot on my team,' in reference to the governors of the BFI. He was quite right, and in some ways I felt closer to the Lancashire Police because at least they were a team; they weren't wishy-washy and they knew exactly what they wanted. *Juvenile Liaison* was a tragedy for me; Joan and I were attacked a lot and on quite a personal level. I stopped believing in liberal organizations almost entirely and it certainly took a number of years for my anger to subside.

What level of interest did the second film provoke?
Very little, actually. I think that in Blackburn Sergeant Ray got hammered all over again, but there was actually very little press interest in it. It wasn't a hot news story like the first one was. The police were also able to say that they had substantially changed the scheme.

It's quite sinister, the way that Sergeant Ray was airbrushed out of the police's history. All your calls to the police enquiring about his whereabouts and his history in the second film lead to a dead end. But then comes a poignant moment where you do manage finally to get him on the phone and he makes the point that he felt that the editing of the film was unfair in that you never show him interacting positively with the families, a role he felt he frequently performed. I guess that editing is a process of manipulation, especially in documentary.
I can't say that I don't feel guilty about Sergeant Ray but I'm not sure that it would come down to the specifics of the editing. The way I edit has progressed a lot since that point, and the yardstick by which I judge something is whether or not I feel that it is fair and accurate in an overall way, and whether or not I feel comfortable with the film. In regard to the scene that Ray was particularly criticized for, the locking up of Glen in the cells, I did enable him to talk in the car about why he had done it, and that interview was specifically done to try and put his actions into context. I think he actually says something along the lines of that being the first time he had taken such actions, and we put that in, specifically to try to redress the balance. It paints him in a more human way. It's so hard because I generally think that Sergeant Ray's heart and soul were good, and within his own vocabulary of behaviour he was a fair man. He really thought that this was the right way to behave and it wasn't at all that he was a sadist or enjoyed putting Glen in the cell. The point is that if he'd been trained in a different way, I'm sure he would have behaved differently.

It's fascinating how in Juvenile Liaison 2 *you show the children from the original film watching how they are treated by Ray and his colleagues. When Glen watches the scene with him in the police cell, he comments that he thinks that it was the right thing for Sergeant Ray to have done as it stopped him from going on and doing worse things. Conversely, in another scene of a family watching back the original footage, a daughter is appalled by the threats of violence her father directed towards her brother.*

I must see the second film again because *Juvenile Liaison* was such a painful episode in the lives of Joan and I that I seem to have blocked the film from my memory. It brought Joan and I a lot closer, but *Juvenile Liaison 2* always felt to me like an apology for the first one not happening and I have only watched it once since it was finished. What was great about *Juvenile Liaison 2* was that the kids were able to answer back, and their thinking was much more progressive than that of their parents.

It's also interesting to look at how your film-making style has changed between the first film and the second; the second film makes much more use of music and the increased presence of yourself within the film, knocking on doors, making phone calls and generally acting as an agent within the framework of the film.

Let me ask you something: did you find the first film a much more intense viewing experience?

I actually found them equally intense. I think that the style of the second film is appropriate to the subject because it is a piece of investigative journalism.

The first film really was the one that propelled me out of the UK. I think that *Juvenile Liaison 2* was the first documentary film I made in the UK since the original *Juvenile Liaison*.

Which factors influenced your going to work in America?

I knew that there was funding in America, Joan was American, there were no manning requirements and independent film-making was so much more alive. You have to remember that this is before Channel Four and before Margaret Thatcher came in and got rid of the ACTT,[2] so all these elements made America very attractive. There was also a romantic attraction to the fact that people like Fred Wiseman worked there.

Both Juvenile Liaisons *films are credited as 'A Film by Nick Broomfield and Joan Churchill.' Your critics describe you as vain, but do you think they overlook your tendency to give credit to your collaborators?*

I think with Joan – even though our roles are very different – we really made the films together and the credit is really a recognition of that and of our partnership. This goes back to what Colin Young was try-ing to achieve at the film school, and Joan has always been my partner in this way. Making a film is a fiery, egocentric thing and – let's put it this way – on every film there are a number of people with enormous amounts to contribute, and without them you couldn't make the film. On later films these people included Michele D'Acosta, Riete Oord and Jo Human, and I had very close relationships with all these peo-ple. Sure, ultimately there is only one director, and I am very strong in the editing room too, so one voice tends to come through strongest. But my collaborators do have a big influence, and I think that the films are not just the journals of my own discoveries but represent the jour-neys that the others working on the film go through too. In a sense, I have developed this public persona and I think that I just have to do what I think is the right thing. Obviously, there are people who con-sider me to be an egomaniac and totally narcissistic, with a burning desire to get in front of the camera. I feel that these people are totally entitled to that opinion but also feel that I know why I am doing the films and why I am making them in that way. Maybe I do have a par-ticular thing that gets up some people's noses, and I do partly regret that and wish that I could do something about it. Maybe it is, as Derek Malcolm said, something in my voice . . .

But your voice is perfect at expressing understatement and bringing humour to the films: as in the Margaret Thatcher film, where you com-ment that your relationship with her press secretary had now deterio-rated visibly.
People sometimes think that the humour is self-satisfied. Other people, such as Michael Moore and Louis Theroux, get accused of the same thing, Michael Moore perhaps less so because of his background.

How much do you suppose the personal relationship you had with Joan impacted upon your working dynamic?
We are very similar people, similar in our interests. I also think that documentary film-makers are a particular breed of people, with curiosity being the determining factor, along with a fascination for things and a willingness to be chameleon-like and to become a part of the situation that you are engulfed in. It's also the diversity of the life that attracts one. One moment you may be staying at the Hotel du Cap in Cannes and the next you find yourself in some shithole in

Blackburn – and you find both experiences as fascinating and amazing in their own way.

Joan is an amazingly stylish and elegant person with an absolute ability to fit in with anyone and draw anybody out and be genuinely interested in anyone. This is what united us more than anything in the beginning. Our son Barney has this ability too. Pennebaker and Wiseman also all have it – a love for their subjects and this capacity to fit in. I think that this was what united Joan and I. What did become difficult was that we were in what I would term 'the front line' together, taking metaphorical bullets for each other. When a day doing this finishes, it becomes hard to switch to romantic mode. And this probably ultimately affected our relationship. Joan is still absolutely my best friend. If I go to a party and Joan is there I will invariably spend the whole evening talking to her just because I still have more to talk to her about than anyone else.

And what about the working relationship once the personal relationship finished? You worked apart for quite some time.
It coincided with the demise of the Lily Tomlin film, which led to the more overt stylistic change in my work – a change that Joan did not initially approve of, but slowly got more used to. A lot of things came to a head. The Lily Tomlin film finished around 1985 and we didn't properly work together again until 1996 on *Kurt and Courtney*. I resumed the working relationship out of despair about halfway through that film, which was very stressful to make. Filming Kurt's friends, who were mainly junkies up in Seattle and Portland, was quite emotionally draining and confusing, and the two cameramen whom I was working with were quite inexperienced; I was quite demanding and that didn't make for a good combination. So, in the middle of the film, I was forced to fire them both, which was fucking scary, leaving me with lots of unpaid bills and equipment that needed to be returned to a rental house that I had absolutely no idea the location of. To fire your crew on a film is a desperately last resort thing to do. I could do it because I was the producer too and so not really answerable to anybody else.

One can't help but notice that almost all of your major collaborators are female.
That's right. I went to a co-educational school and perhaps conse-

quently my closest friends have almost always been women. I also have male friends, but I probably relax more with women. Opposites also attract, and I think that with film crews it works much better to have mixed-sex crews.

You've mentioned your admiration for fellow documentary film-makers, but they have almost exclusively been American. What about British directors such as John Grierson[3] and Humphrey Jennings?[4]
A lot of those films are kind of like feature films that have been made in studios – *Night Mail* (1936) and so on – and are not really what I would call documentary. Robert Flaherty is another one whom I find slightly too theatrical. I like films to be real in the sense that they are unscripted and have an immediacy, an uncertainty and a rawness to them. This is the magic for me. Somebody like Paul Rotha[5] is much closer to the kind of documentary film-maker I like. I have to be honest and say that I was never crazy about Humphrey Jennings; he just didn't move my heart. Another film I should mention that I love is called *Horse of Mud* (1971) by the female Egyptian film-maker Ateyyat El Abnoudy. Other key films I like would include *Sherman's March* (1986) by Ross McElwee, *Home from the Hills* (1985) by Molly Dineen and *Song of Ceylon* (1934) by Basil Wright, a film that was produced by Grierson's documentary movement.

And where do you stand on Michael Moore as a film-maker? His Fahrenheit 9/11 *looks set to become the biggest documentary of all time[6] and seems to have galvanized people into seeing documentaries again.*
I think that Michael Moore is a pamphleteer in a way. His films are very structured; they are certainly not long and meandering, and so are perhaps less concerned with the immediacy of the moment. Moore sets what I call elephant traps; he lays elaborate traps and then films the aftermath, which is a delicious thing to do, and Moore is particularly brilliant at it. I admire him and his work. I've also from time to time employed the elephant-trap technique, for example with Eugene Terre'Blanche in *The Leader, His Driver and the Driver's Wife*, when I deliberately turned up late for his interview. I certainly knew the kind of reaction it would get and went out of my way to induce it. This was one of those rare moments of bravery on my part; sometimes there are things that you know are not meant to pass you by and that you

would be a coward more than brave not to do them. Cowardice is very appealing a lot of the time . . .

Notes

1. The winner of the Grierson Memorial Trust 2003 Trustees' Award for outstanding contribution to the art of documentary, Molly Dineen's films include: *Heart of the Angel* (1989), *The Ark* (1993), *Tony Blair* (1997), *Geri* (1999) and *The Lord's Tale* (2002).
2. Association of Cinematograph Technicians.
3. Considered a founding father of the British documentary movement of the thirties, John Grierson started the Empire Marketing Board (EMB) Film Unit and, in 1933, the GPO Film Unit. Under Grierson's watchful eye films such as *Drifters* (1929), *Industrial Britain* (1933), *Song of Ceylon* (1934) and *Night Mail* (1936) emerged. At the start of the war Grierson was appointed Canadian Film Commissioner and founded the National Film Board of Canada. In 1951 he became Executive Producer of Group Three, a production unit that was designed to make quality programme fillers.
4. Considered amongst the finest cinematic achievements of the World War II period in Britain, the films of Humphrey Jennings are an intrinsic part of the British wartime cinema scene. Joining the GPO documentary unit in 1934 as a designer and editor, Jennings began to direct his own films with titles such as *Locomotives* (1934) and *Night Mail* (1936). Arguably his masterwork is the montage-inspired *Fires Were Started* (1943), a look at the conditions faced by London's wartime firemen.
5. A leading documentarist who joined John Grierson back in the days of the Empire Marketing Board. Paul Rotha also wrote a number of basic film books, including *The Film Till Now* and *Documentary Film*. His documentaries include: *Desert Outpost* (1937), *Total War in Britain* (1946), *Land of Promise* (1946), *Cradle of Genius* (1961) and *The Life of Adolf Hitler* (1961). Like Broomfield, Rotha also made a foray into fiction film-making with *No Resting Place* (1950).
6. At the time of writing, Michael Moore's *Fahrenheit 9/11* has grossed £5.6 million in the UK and $113 million in the US. Commercially, it has become the most successful documentary in history.

3

Coming to America

Tattooed Tears, Soldier Girls, Chicken Ranch,
Lily Tomlin, Driving Me Crazy

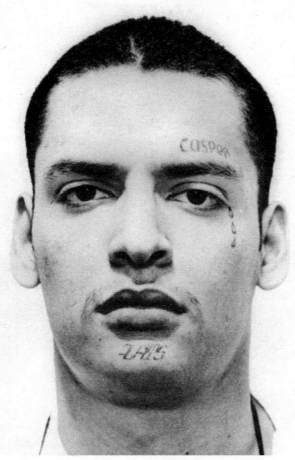

Casper, one tear-drop for each year, *Tatooed Tears*

Buck being severely restrained,
Tattooed Tears

Broomfield's first American documentary, Tattooed Tears *is a series of case studies of the inmates of the California Youth Authority Prison in Chino, California. Reputedly there for rehabilitation, the film reveals how the prisoners are actually forced to undergo vindictive punishment, accruing extra time for petty institutional misdemeanours. Allegedly a liberal regime, the overriding atmosphere is of an intense and frequently humiliating brutality.*

NB: *Tattooed Tears* was a progression from *Juvenile Liaison* and was all to do with the question of justice and juveniles. It was more a series of case studies, whereas my second American film, *Soldier Girls*, followed a more complicated structure, interweaving stories during the process of basic military training. *Tattooed Tears* is a progression in that it is case studies of particular inmates and a little bit of a-day-in-the-life-type activity as well. The film really looks at the idea of whether life at the institution is to do with rehabilitation or whether it is really just a holding facility. It looks at various cases and raises questions as to whether people require more psychiatric attention and whether some of the inmates are more affected by the institution itself than by their initial crime, which is often very insignificant. In fact, many of the inmates pick up so much time when they are at the institution that they are like hardened criminals when they come out.

JW: *I was shocked by the case of Brian, who was admitted for a very minor misdemeanour but then ended up staying a very long time.*
He was originally admitted for firing a BB gun, but had a very volatile temper and picked up a lot of extra time for discipline infractions. One of the positive things that came out of the film was that there was a

review of the sentencing procedures and the film got the Californian state bar award because they changed the rules regarding the parole board's ability to give inmates more time for these disciplinary infractions.

I think that all of these films are to do with the extent to which we are part of a caring society that is trying to alleviate and make a problem better rather than compounding it by the way that people are treated within those institutions. I think that the Youth Training School had been set up with the best possible intentions but had become unjust in that the weaker inmates, who were being bullied and so were often just defending themselves, accrued a lot of extra time.

How did the guards treat the inmates? There seemed to be a lot of racially motivated provocation, so I wondered about the general atmosphere of brutality.
It reminds me of what is happening in Iraq today, in that there is a thick skin that you very quickly assume. It's a protection for everybody who's there against the horror of what is happening on a daily basis. There were several inmates who were stabbed to death while we were filming and numerous gang killings. Very quickly a morbid humour developed to deal with it. There were a number of people there, such as Pedro, who hallucinated and saw things. I remember one inmate saw a train that would regularly come through his cell. The reaction of the superintendent was, 'Well, as long as the train doesn't stop and he doesn't get on it we're OK.'

The film was also shot at a time when the Mexican mafia, which I wasn't able to go into so much, was using a lot of the younger inmates to commit murders out on the streets and these murders were then reciprocated within the institution. The authorities didn't want me to get into that too much, but this was creating the heaviest tension. I think this situation has now got worse, largely due to drugs. It was also shocking to find that the white inmates would pretty much have to join the Aryan brotherhood for protection.

The film opens by quoting state policy: 'The state of California does not believe in rehabilitating young offenders, only punishing them.' This gives little hope to those being held there.
It was a very brutal place and threw me back very much on myself. Both Joan and I nearly got raped when we were making the film, Joan

Nick gets his one phone call,
Tattooed Tears

inside this enormous walk-in fridge where the panic button didn't work, while I had a very bad encounter in one of the units. We both found the shoot really draining, both in terms of being subjected to the hopelessness and brutality of the institution and because of the daily abuse that we had to suffer. It was very depressing being there day after day, so God knows what it must have been like for a prisoner. I was very affected by it and I do remember that, whenever we would try to take time off from filming, an incident would always happen that we should have filmed, and you realize that it is better just to stay there so that the actual shoot would, in effect, go quicker. We would sleep in the prison hospital in case anything happened at night, so in effect we were prisoners ourselves. It was a terribly desperate place.

There are constant incidents of the inmates finding cockroaches in their food.
The place was intolerable, but it's funny how quickly we as a crew became immune to stuff that went on. When you first go to prison you are quite open to having discussions with the prisoners, but then you begin to doubt everybody because almost everyone there will claim that they are there incorrectly, that they didn't do what they are

65

charged with, and very quickly, like the staff there, you become immune to their stories. It is a depressing fact of human nature, but you do become desensitized. Human nature is all about survival and getting on with your own life and functioning as well as possible.

When we started making the film we originally had an assistant called Barry Wilson who had a freak-out during the making of the film. He had previously been Joan's assistant on *Punishment Park* (1971),[1] and he ended up going back to England. The environment was so difficult because abuse would continually be hurled at you. This was made even more difficult for me by being Joan's boyfriend at the time because sexual comments were constantly directed at Joan. Also, because Joan was operating the camera I had to carry all the equipment in what looked like a pram, so it seemed like I was in the female submissive position while Joan got to carry the big phallic camera. I was known as the 'faggot Englander', which after three months became wearying. They also used to slap my backside, the ultimate prison insult.

Despite the almost impenetrable air of brutality, there are some sympathetic members of staff. One of the governors of the board empathizes with the inmate subjected to the rectum search and tries to defend him against occurring more incidental time for his resistance.
But, in general, there really wasn't much hope and there was no delusion that people were being taught there. It was just a holding pen. Look at how ridiculous the lectures were. One lecturer talks about how great America is because we can eat steak, unlike in the communist countries. The lectures actually give the impression that America has stopped believing in itself.

It's also depressing the way the inmates learn. They are sat in front of arcane television programmes to perform the most mundane tasks.
It's very disrespectful and the whole thing was so lethargic.

The issue of rape is not something that comes across particularly clearly from the film, although one inmate, Pedro, is known to have been sexually abused.
It was a constant occurrence and a constant threat. But including this in the film was tricky. For example, we did shoot footage involving a rape victim and his rapist talking about the rape, but I decided not to

include it because I really did feel that it was material that could affect the rest of the victim's life, who at the time was only fifteen or sixteen years old. In a way, there were so many secrets in that institution that weren't really accessible by a straight *cinema vérité* film, but this wasn't really the film that we were making; in strict terms it is a *cinema vérité* piece. Nothing was staged, for example, and everything we caught was absolutely genuine. We weren't able to capture how the gangs operated, didn't really get to see how drugs were trafficked into the institution and the extent to which people were gang-raped and so on. I do hope, however, that the style in which the film is made does give a real feel for the institution and its many horrors.

Were you granted unlimited access?
We were. In fact, we were given the keys.

You said that the film was influenced by Fred Wiseman. Did you ever show it to him?
I did. I showed it to him in his wonderful editing room located on a wharf in Boston. I think he liked it. We did have to use some form of lighting – a sun gun located on one of the cameras – because the stock at this time wasn't fast enough and the prison was very dark, and I think Fred had reservations about this aspect. I liked this lighting approach as it contributed to the sinister atmosphere. My own attitude to the film is that it is quite unrelenting and it is quite hard for me to sit through, partly because it brings back a very painful experience.

It does seem to end on a note of hope when we hear that Brian achieves his dream of leaving the institution and going to college. But then I think the very final image is of another inmate, Ronnie, chained to the cell bars like an animal.
It's interesting to consider – if one was doing the film again – whether one would adopt a different approach and, for me, *Tattooed Tears* is a particularly humourless film in comparison to my later works. It tends to operate only in one gear and it hits the audience emotionally but not on any other level. There is humour, even if only gallows humour, in every situation, and the advantage of this is that it allows the audience to recover a bit and you have more impact when you delve into the next story of despair.

On your website you list a number of reviews of the film and Tattooed Tears *is widely praised both as a piece of* cinema vérité *and for raising the levels of the intolerable. I was just wondering if your reviews are something to which you pay a great deal of attention?*
Not really. It's more important to consider what you feel about it as an artist and whether you feel that there is progression between projects. There is certainly progression between something like this and *Soldier Girls*, which I believe to be a much more finely balanced film; it's like a concerto in a way, with different moods and so on. *Tattooed Tears* is certainly the darkest film I have made. It's rather like Dante's inferno, though in its own way completely accurate. But, afterwards, I certainly felt the need to do something different.

How did the title suggest itself?
Joan and I were going to call it *California Youth Authority* but there was this wonderful orange-ranch owner who lived in Ojai, California, a Mr Cahoun, and I was buying a 1955 Chevy off of him. Mr Cahoun was a real gentleman, in his late eighties, with a really philosophical nature about him. During negotiations for the car he asked me what I was doing, and I told him about the film. He asked me the title so that he could look out for it, and when I told him, 'California Youth Authority,' he replied, 'That is the worst title I have ever heard.' He was adamant that we needed a better one and so asked me to describe some scenes from the film so that he could ruminate. He claimed to be good at titles and, to be honest, I thought, 'Oh yeah,' but decided to humour him. Joan and I described some sequences and early the next morning we called him. He told us that he had been up half the night but had finally came up with something: *Tattooed Tears*. I had to admit that it was genius. His car was also great. I had it from 1978 to 2000, when it sadly got stolen. The only problem with the car, which I eventually gave to Barney, was its inability to stop.

Broomfield followed Tattooed Tears *with a look at another American institution. Shot at Fort Gordon, Georgia,* Soldier Girls *follows the members of a young female platoon as they undergo induction and basic military training. Put through their paces by the fearsome and fiercely intelligent Sergeant Abing – a Vietnam veteran with seemingly little tolerance of women in the army – the largely observational film examines the patriarchal structure of institutions and the brutalizing nature of the US army.*

As I mentioned, *Tattooed Tears* had led to a review of sentencing procedures within the institution, and I think Joan and I wanted to do something about the way in which people were conditioned and trained in different institutions. We looked at various different institutions, including a number of police academies. Joan's mother is very closely associated with the LAPD, which is a paramilitary police force that employs a lot of the tactics that are now being used in London, and we were very interested in doing something there, but we couldn't get access to them, partly perhaps because of Joan's background. Each of these investigations took a couple of months, so then, in despair, we decided to take a VW camper and drive across the country, something I have always wanted to do anyway. I remember that we went and spent some time on the Four Corners Indian reservation, where there was a lot of mining for plutonium going on, but we just had the feeling that the Indians so disliked the white race that we shouldn't do it, that it should be an Indian who did something on the subject.

Then we drove down into Carolina and Georgia and, while we were there, by chance we were in a postcard shop and saw all these postcards of women in uniform bayoneting straw dummies and wearing shit-eating grins on their faces; it was a very funny image. We both thought that it would be so interesting because not only is it about the changing role of women within society, but it would also be interesting to look at that training process. So we contacted the Pentagon and I remember going there in our best suits and we were met by this person called Major Sliger, who was quite an attractive Californian woman who looked so disappointed by the sight of us in our natty outfits, but she did give us access to any of the bases that we wanted to film at. Almost as soon as we got to Fort Gordon in Georgia we met Sergeant Abing, who would become one of our main characters. We saw him working with Private Johnson, the girl with the wonderful grin that Abing was constantly trying to get rid of. We actually shot for about a week at Fort Dix, but the characters weren't as interesting and also it was right by a big military airport so the noise was terrible. While we were filming there I kept thinking about Sergeant Abing and Joanne Johnson and then just decided to leave. We drove back to Fort Gordon and literally started shooting the moment we got there.

Were you surprised at how open the Pentagon was in allowing this access?

From left to right, Tutin, Hall and Johnson,
Soldier Girls

American institutions, on the whole, are very open. The fact that they are funded by taxpayers' money has led to an ingrained belief in the public's right to know. There is also a much greater freedom of the press than there is in this country; institutions in the States are just more publicly accountable than they are in the UK. I think that we are a much more secretive society because we are a much older democracy, in a sense. America is very upfront and, certainly on paper, is a much more vigorous democracy in that the rights of the media are actually written into the constitution.

And what was it about Sergeant Abing that particularly interested you? He reminds one of the drill instructor in Kubrick's Full Metal Jacket *(1987).*[2]
I have it on good authority from Andrew Braunsberg, who knew

Sergeant Abing laying down the law to
Private Johnson, *Soldier Girls*

Kubrick, that he saw *Soldier Girls* and was influenced by Abing. Sergeant Abing was a very complicated character. He was obviously much more educated than the average drill sergeant and had been to college and wrote poetry. He was also a very conflicted human being who had been inducted into the marines for the Vietnam War and, I think, had been a reluctant crew member. He'd had his nose and a few other things broken in training, but they made him into a very effective killer; he was one of those soldiers that was sent into the jungle with piano wire and was very haunted by his demons. In the evening when he got drunk he would play a terrifying game with a knife in-between his hands. At first I thought he was just a sadist, but when I got to know him it was hard not to sympathize with him. Which is why we put that scene at the end of the film.

This is when he says that he 'can't love any more' and that war 'has robbed him of his humanity' – a sequence that certainly ends the film on a different note.
I wanted the viewer to review everything that they had just watched; this was something that I was going to leave them with. I think it's very easy

71

to adopt an opinion about people in those positions – whether it's jailers, policemen, soldiers – and it's very rare that one actually thinks about the fact that they may have been brutalized, that their humanity has been stripped away. I think that, taking this into account, you have to review the whole process and come up with answers as to how, in order to amend the situation, there have to be fundamental changes, because the process of putting somebody in that position inevitably brings out the worst. Sergeant Abing was certainly somebody who was struggling with his humanity in a totally inhuman situation. At other times he would say things like, 'You can't teach someone to kill nicely,' and would really brutalize his recruits on the basis that that is the situation in which the recruits would find themselves should they ever go into war, and, in a way, he was absolutely correct.

Was he intimidating towards yourself and Joan during the film?
No, not at all. In fact, we grew quite close to Sergeant Abing, but when the film came out we couldn't get hold of him because the Pentagon was then very against the film and forbade a number of their libraries on training bases to buy it, even though a number of them wanted to use it. It was a bit like Sergeant Ray all over again in that Abing was given a very hard time, and it was only years later when Joan was in Madison, Wisconsin, that she got hold of him after finding him in the phone book. He had just left the army, and they met up and he still hadn't seen the film. Joan showed it to him, and he was very moved. By this time he had a family and a young daughter. When Joan got back to Los Angeles she opened her suitcase to find that he had put in his Purple Heart, his highest decoration and one of his proudest possessions. This was about six or seven years ago.

You said that you wanted to look at the position of women in society and within institutions. What did you find? The expression of emotion seemed to be frowned upon.
Well, I suppose that in the army there is little room for emotion. You give an order and people do what you tell them to do. There's no debating an order. Oddly enough, the women were much better shots than the men and achieved much higher marksmanship scores because they followed instructions better than the men. A lot of the men felt that they were natural shots because they had been out shooting deer or whatever. Because a lot of the women were going to end up in sig-

nals and communications, a lot of them were going to be very close to the front line and so would be prime targets. Though I believe that Sergeant Abing thought that women shouldn't be in the army, I think he felt that, if they were going to be, then he would make sure that they received as good a training as they could. This is not to say that I felt that all his training methods were just. I think that Sergeant Abing, like the other sergeants, was just a bit nuts. There was that institutionalized nuttiness that naturally happens when there is a lot of emotion and very little contact with the outside world; that's very apparent in a number of the scenes with Alves and the very irrational dislike of Johnson – particularly odd given that Johnson was the best-educated recruit.

This irrationality often manifests itself as brutality and victimization. Alves is carted off to a dormitory on her own and threatened with a visit to a psychiatrist.

Alves almost became the enemy. I think that institutions are so insular and inward-looking that they have the propensity to do that. This is very clear from Kubrick's *Full Metal Jacket*, which also reveals the process of making a person into a soldier who will quite blindly follow orders as a brutalizing one.

The other problem with an institution like the army is that people start off on an even footing but quite quickly rank is assigned. Again, Alves suffers because of this when one of her fellow privates is made a squad leader and dispenses punishment to her.

It's like two little girls, really. They have been given this ludicrous task of digging a grave for 'Marvin', Sergeant Abing's helmet liner, and platoon leader Hall starts to give Alves real grief. Alves does not take at all well to it and, rather as if they are in the playground, tells her to lay off. The difference is that these people have weapons and are licensed to kill but emotionally have barely left home. We really liked Hall, but there was an element of the Hitler youth to her in that she was so gung-ho and so motivated that there is no stopping her. You could see this terrible abuse of power unfolding but, in a way, this is exactly what the army wants.

Johnson and Tutin frequently giggle together in an infectious and conspiratorial manner and became, for me, the most endearing of the

recruits. Were these the two that you and Joan were also closest to?
I think so. There were a lot of girls that came into the army because there simply wasn't any other work in places like Mississippi, where the majority of them were from. America is a very unfit country: people drive everywhere in their cars and are generally very unphysical, so it was a big shock for a lot of these women. Johnson and Tutin were great fun and really enjoyed life and, as with most of the women, couldn't believe that they were suddenly asked to perform all these arduous tasks and exercises. They used to have these runs and they forced Joan to go on one of them too, and it was interesting that she was so far ahead of all the others despite being fifteen years older than most of them. All the recruits also insisted that we accompany them on the route marches, even though our equipment was much heavier than theirs. They were party girls and just wanted a good life and had no intention of killing anyone. The army was just a way of getting out of their small towns and seeing something of the rest of the world.

There is only one short scene where two privates discuss why they joined up. Did you not want more of these discussions?
I felt that what we were doing there was more a psychological portrait of them and their training and who they were. You certainly get a sense that these are people from pretty low-income groups who don't have any innate patriotic zeal to join the army and they are certainly not great athletes endowed with a strong fighting spirit. It's quite clear that this is probably their only option. If you are working within a particular style – and again this is a very observational, *cinema vérité* piece – you have to go with what you get and you can't create scenes. I think that it worked well in that situation because you get a strong sense of the emotions. Interview is fine and it works well, but it is an intervention of the film-maker to get what he wants to talk about as opposed to what the subjects are talking about.

Given the bulky equipment, the fact that you were marching in the suffocating heat, the shoot must have been hellish.
It was. We filmed for fourteen weeks and Georgia at that time of year was unbearably hot. To combat this, training would start at 5.30 in the morning and finish by 11; you literally couldn't walk because the humidity ensured that you were enveloped in sweat. We were certainly very fit by the end of shooting and I quite enjoyed that aspect. I pre-

fer to do something that is physically demanding as opposed to just sitting around in someone's office waiting for stuff to happen. There were a lot of constraints in that there was a motel on the base but you could only stay in it for five days at a time because they were trying to stop the families of the soldiers from just moving into the motel permanently; so every five days we would have to pack up all our equipment, move off base for a night or two and then go back. This became really tiresome.

The roll call of the recruits at the start of the film reminds me of the credits on Dad's Army.
This is the kind of effect we wanted. We wanted it to be more like a soap, and we wanted to reflect that the piece was a little like a feature film in that it offered character studies. It was the last film that I did with Joan in this style.

In terms of contemporary politics, it's interesting to note that within the film the Middle East has replaced communism as the American focal point of hatred. One of the military chants is 'I want to kill an Iranian.'
There was a feeling that the politicians were holding the army back, that America could have taken Vietnam any time it wanted to but the politicians were cowed by political considerations instead of giving the army full reign to do what it wanted to do. The army was still smarting from that and the humiliation of defeat and of not being accepted back into society as heroes. You have to remember that most of the drill sergeants had served in Vietnam.

Abing actually does a speech in which he states, 'We didn't lose that war.'
They were very much the Republican gung-ho – and I'm tempted to say white-trash – type, but in the process of making the film I surprisingly found myself liking a lot of these people. I certainly didn't think I would, and one of the joys of making these films is that you get to know people first-hand who – maybe philosophically and politically – you fundamentally disagree with, but as human beings you find them wonderful. I remember feeling, as I did with *Juvenile Liaison*, that in many ways you identify far more closely with the police or the army than you do with lily-livered liberals who can't make their mind up about anything and are the worst support team to have because they

can't agree on any kind of direction. The army was enormous fun to hang out with and it was interesting to see the ideology of these people from within, as extreme and bigoted as it was in some cases.

It's hard, though, for the viewer to have any affinity with the sergeants in the film, particularly after watching their shocking hostility towards Alves.

I think they had come from incredibly brutalized backgrounds and had themselves been through an incredibly bruising conflict. They were largely uneducated, they hadn't received any proper training and they mostly let rip. They have an authority that they probably shouldn't have, and I think that if you look at the breakdown that has happened in Iraq at the moment with the stories of torture,[3] this stems from an assumption within the institutions that this is an acceptable way to behave. I'm sure that Fort Gordon is not an isolated case regarding the bullying of recruits by sergeants. Of course, when we see this behaviour in our more rarefied, educated world we are rightly horrified by it, but they simply don't have this point of reference. In a perverse way, there is perhaps more honesty regarding the way that they are because what you see is what you get. Everybody has demons and, quite often, the more sophisticated you are the more capable you are of sorting them out or of filtering them off into other things. That's also one of the by-products of education, and these people just didn't have that.

I think that Sergeant Abing was different in that he had sophistication and insight which, in a sense, made his time in the army more difficult because he didn't really know quite where to put himself. He is also quite poetic, even in terms of the way he speaks. I recall the way he says to Alves, 'That's why we are going to send you to a psychiatrist, to sort out that little mad maze you call a mind.' That's genius; he is a very great orator and also very funny. I also think that a lot of what he does is very tongue-in-cheek, to entertain himself as much as anything else. He assumes the position of the ogre but I'm not sure that he really thinks that of himself.

He seems also to reserve a particular dislike for Johnson.

He thought that Johnson was just a fuck-up. Interestingly, Johnson was, like him, the most educated of her group and so was probably the closest match for him. She was also, like Abing, very witty and just had it down; she was on the nail and could out-fox him. This made her much more of

76

a threat than anybody else. Johnson also understood their psychology, knew where they came from, and as a result had complete contempt for them. She was, in her own way, a rebel who was undermining their authority, and this was something that they just couldn't accept.

Were there ever accusations of racism? Johnson and Tutin, the other recruit whose life Abing makes very difficult, are both black.
I'm sure that there was racism in the American army and I found it interesting that, when Johnson was falling behind in the road march, it was a black sergeant who picked her up and gave her a run-down of the history of the US and his own history of coming from slave stock. This racism is ingrained in the South too, but I certainly don't think that Abing was an overt racist. A lot of the other drill sergeants were far worse and were close to being in the Klan. The US army also has a long tradition of using the blacks as cannon fodder and never promoting them, and these elements are certainly still there.

One of the most amazing scenes in the film is where a sergeant, during survival training, tears the head off a live chicken with his teeth.
I'd heard about this act, but I was still slightly surprised when we filmed

Soldier Girls cartoon that appeared in *Punch*

it. Apparently they used to also do it with rabbits but had been unable to get a live rabbit that day. As a film-maker you are in a double bind because you hear about these things and encourage them to happen because it is a really important scene for the film, but you also hate the death of the chicken. Apparently, the rabbit, which the sergeant would skin alive, would have a more emotional effect on the recruits, which is no doubt why the rabbit was the preferred animal for the demonstration.

It's quite an emotional moment when Johnson is finally ejected from the army and, after bidding farewell to all her colleagues, kisses Joan and yourself goodbye.
We really liked Johnson. I thought that she was a genuinely kind person with an amazing sense of humour. Joan and I were both very sad to see her go and, in fact, Joan's reaction was very emotional. We had become so much a part of the environment and so much a part of the platoon that we shared many of their daily habits. For example, we would get up at the same time as them and did their training with them all day. Of course, we developed particular relationships with those we liked and Johnson was probably our favourite.

And what effect did the dynamic between Joan and yourself have? Did you find that the recruits related more to Joan and the sergeants to yourself?
A lot of the women related on a more intimate level to Joan. I think they liked me but were also quite curious. I had a similar effect on the drill sergeants; they quite liked me but couldn't figure out who I was. Joan is a very empathetic person because she is such a good listener. People like to talk to her; she is genuinely very interested in people and likes to help them, and people quite quickly sense that. I'm often a lot more disciplined and more worried about what the fuck is happening with the film. In a sense, I've always been dependent on people like Joan to establish the intimate relationships that help these films get made. Joan and I made *Soldier Girls* together; we co-directed, co-edited and went through the whole shoot together.

I understand that the money ran out during the filming and at one stage you didn't have the funds to complete it.
This has been the case with a number of the films I've done. I've quite often set out with only enough money to actually shoot the film. I

always think that the most important thing is to shoot the film while the window of opportunity is there. You have to have faith in your belief, shoot the film and then go about getting completion money, which is actually often much easier to get.

Who provided the completion money in this instance?
We got a couple of scenes processed and showed them to the Corporation for Public Broadcasting, the funding arm for public broadcasting. They gave us, I think, another $100,000, enough to do the rest of the edit and make a combined print.

How did D. A. Pennebaker and Chris Hegedus assist with the film? Their names are in the credits.
When we had initially shot the film, we used their editing rooms. Fred Wiseman also lent us his sound equipment. What is wonderful about documentary film-makers is that, even though we may be competing for the same money, I've always found, with a few exceptions, that documentarists are always very helpful to each other. It's kind of like a big family, united by curiosity, endless adventures and a general interest in things. Documentary film-makers are by and large, a great group of people who normally go out of their way to help with equipment, funding or even providing a place for each other to stay. For me, it came especially from Pennebaker, Wiseman and Leacock, whereas Joan was especially close to the Maysles.[4] The first documentary film-maker to help me was Sir Arthur Elton. He got me my first bunch of completion money, and gestures like this make one want to carry on in this tradition. When I get people writing to me for help, I always try to, as I remember very distinctly that on several occasions I would have been fucked without the help of others.

You said earlier that you didn't pay too much attention to reviews, but I note that Amanda Spake called Soldier Girls *a 'feminist and humanist triumph'.[5] Does this mean a lot to you?*
Well, yes. I'm not sure at the time that the word 'humanist' meant that much to me but it's probably the concept that I think is the most important. As a documentary, *Soldier Girls* is a celebration of humanity in all its variations; it doesn't take a straight line, so it gives quite a complicated portrait of all the people involved. That's what these films can do and in a way that's quite hard for any other medium to do: to show an

embodiment of contradictions and how a situation or a mood can change so quickly, sometimes in the middle of a shot. Again I think that this is something that I am indebted to Colin Young for, as he was so interested in the way in which decisions come about; he encouraged long takes, so that a scene should almost be just one or two takes, rather than a hotchpotch put together. That encourages one to see the richness of the situation so that you are not only interested in the final result but also at how the final result is achieved. It's a particular way of looking at and understanding people and is a technique that I feel works particularly well in *Soldier Girls*. A lot of the scenes are amazingly shot by Joan and are incredibly cinematic. It's a film that I am very proud of. It's much more of a complicated statement than something like *Tattooed Tears*, as it has such a range of emotions. You also understand the values and training processes of the US army, which was in itself a bundle of contradictions. The characters are also very well-rounded, and I feel that it is very close to our experience of being at Fort Gordon.

A thought-provoking, observational study of legal prostitution in Nevada, Chicken Ranch *is one of Broomfield's first forays into sexual mores as it looks at the girls working at the brothel, their various stories and the domineering attentions of ranch-owner Walter and his premier maid, Fran.*

On Chicken Ranch *you have a new collaborator in Sandi Sissel. How did this relationship come into being?*
Joan was pregnant at the time and about to have Barney, so she wasn't physically able to do the film. Joan and Sandi were friends, and I thought that it was important that this film have a camerawoman. Having said that, I've never had so many offers from cameramen as I did then – I remember even Haskell Wexler[6] and Chris Menges[7] offered to shoot the film, but I thought that a combination of a two-man crew would end in absolute disaster.

It would have exhausted the production funds very quickly.
Exactly, especially as I remember ranch-owner Walter saying, 'Nobody gets anything for free . . .' Again, I felt that it needed somebody who could talk to the women and get to know them. The thing that the girls found hardest to believe was that we weren't making a pornographic film and that we weren't exploiting them. After all, these were people who had been pretty much exploited all their lives and

Welcome to the Chicken Ranch

From left to right: Joey, unknown, Connie, Mandy
Cissy, Diane and Linda, *Chicken Ranch*

81

some were from backgrounds not that dissimilar to Aileen Wuornos.

Initially, we spent three weeks watching the daytime soaps and trying to persuade the working girls at the ranch to take part because at first everyone was reluctant. They were suspicious and couldn't see that there was anything in it for them. They were used to doing a transaction with people and then seeing money as a result, and we weren't offering them anything other than being in the film.

How did you convince them to take part?
I remember – and this was in the days well before cell phones – that there was this rather surreal phone box in the middle of the desert that was invariably engulfed by bugs and I called my mother up, who was quite ill at the time, and complained to her that I was at a loose end and unable to persuade anyone to take part in the film. She said, 'Nick, they're prostitutes, offer them some money!' I think we offered them a really nominal amount of around $200, which was the first time I had paid anybody anything. To me, it was such an alien idea but immediately the majority of the women signed up. There is this idea in documentary that you are losing your integrity if you pay someone – and that is perfectly understandable – but you are dealing here with a culture which is all to do with money and which is all to do with maximizing profit, and people rate themselves entirely on their hourly rate; in some ways, this is the only value that they have and it almost becomes a sign of respect that you think they are worthy of payment. They didn't see themselves as being exploited; in fact, they only saw themselves as being exploited when they weren't being paid.

The idea of paying people to participate in documentaries has become a very topical issue again due to the furore surrounding Nicholas Philibert's Être et avoir (2002).[8]
I do feel that if people are giving up a lot of their time and you are in their houses, using their electricity and their food, then you need to make it all right. We had to pay Walter a facility fee, a nominal amount for a room where we could keep our equipment. This lead to the obvious question: then why should everybody not be paid something? It's down to the individual film-maker. Any situation can be abused, including paying people as a bribe to get them to do or even say something that they ordinarily wouldn't. I think that then you have a real problem regarding the authenticity of what you are getting, but I certainly don't

think that this was the situation with *Chicken Ranch*.

And how difficult was it to persuade the paying customers to take part?
Well, we certainly didn't offer to pay them. It would have been stepping over the mark to offer the trick a blow job on us in order to get them to take part. The customers were very difficult to get; we approached countless customers and, in the end, maybe had about four who would contribute. I think that the only reason we got these was because Walter was in prison at the time, otherwise he would have prevented us from approaching the customers in case it frightened them away.

What was Walter in prison for?
I think it was a violation of some offence regarding the ordinance of the brothel. He was later charged with the murder of a number of girls out in the desert from the time when he had a truck stop there. They were very serious charges from the FBI, but he had a heart attack and died on the eve of the trial.

So we could only approach people if Walter wasn't around. We got to know the pilot who would bring some of the people in by plane, so we would ask him if he would ask the customers on our behalf. The people that drove up to the chicken ranch we would ask as soon as they got through the door, and most of them said no. There was just the odd one or two who agreed to it. People have changed with the advent of television reality shows and the inexhaustible appetite to appear on television no matter what. I certainly think that people would take part more readily now.

Inside the ranch you have the model for a pretty fucked-up family with Walter as the father, the protective maid Fran as the mother and the girls, who are like the children.
I think that the film created more of that feeling than actually existed there. Because we were making a film, we needed obviously to create a certain continuity of characters than there was in reality. There was a great turnover of girls and many of them, who were on drugs, were very fly-by-night and would zoom in and then just as quickly zoom out again after staying a couple of days and getting involved in an argument.

There were actually three maids, including Fran. Fran had previously been a madam, but she'd had a falling out with Walter, who then took her back on as one of the three maids. I thought that it would be too confusing to have three maids so I somewhat falsely created Fran as this mother figure, which she certainly wanted to be. We gave her authority, in a sense, and tried to get her on as many shifts as possible. I think that by virtue of us making the film, a number of the girls who liked us stayed working at the ranch longer than they ordinarily would have done. It's a pretty lonely existence in those caravans, just waiting for someone to come through, and when we were around there was a lot more fun and something of a party atmosphere.

The film doesn't make the ranch look so bad. There is a party, and you do get the sense that Fran really cares about the women. In one scene she dispenses advice to a woman who is thinking of taking off with a man Fran warns could be a potential pimp. However, as the film goes on you see that it is not a pleasant environment at all and that Walter is actually a physically threatening bully.

Walter was a really fucked-up person. Like so many people that I have met in a number of different situations, he was one of those types who believed that he was the same person that he was when he was twenty-one. Somewhere deep inside, Walter believed that he was a decent guy, and I think that there was a part of him that wanted to be a decent guy, but he took a lot of pills and became corrupted. He was always having affairs with the girls, a pollution of business ethics that I guess must be something of a temptation when you are running a brothel.

Nick, Fran and Sandi Sissel,
Chicken Ranch

Walter and one of the girls,
Chicken Ranch

My personal view was that he probably was responsible for the earlier murders so really was quite evil. He certainly instituted a reign of terror at the ranch, with rumours that girls were being recorded and that he had various girls acting as informants for him. There was a real paranoia at the ranch that was no doubt partly pill-induced.

Was it a terribly difficult shoot?
It was. Sandi had an especially tough time and struggled halfway through the film. Walter wanted to chuck us out at one point, so I invented a ruse to keep us there. The ruse involved a proposed piece on the film in the *LA Times*, and as Walter loved publicity he allowed us to stay on an extra couple of weeks to finish the film.

These films, especially when they are so enclosed, do put a massive strain on a person beyond their technical abilities. Human skills, mental stability and endurance are demanded, as opposed to just getting the camera operation right. I hadn't worked with Sandi before and I think we only got through this by the skin of our teeth. Sandi mainly shoots features now and perhaps that is a medium to which she is more suited.

Things do look like they are about to spiral out of control at the end of the film. You interview one of the girls, Mandy, after she has been brutalized by Walter and you get the sense that she genuinely fears for her safety. Thereafter, Walter becomes quite physical towards you and makes it clear in no uncertain terms that he wants you to cease filming and will take any film that you continue to shoot from you. Could the situation there have escalated out of control?

Well, Walter had a gun and I think that Walter, his son and another guy got involved as they were cruising for a fight. For reasons a psychiatrist would no doubt find interesting, I am often at my calmest at moments like that. I wasn't terribly worried, though in hindsight I should have been. When this was happening I remember saying to our friend Christine Burril, who was acting as the journalist from the *LA Times*, that she should get the car and keep it running at the front of the brothel so that we could make a quick getaway once we were in the car with our equipment. Sandi was brilliant in that she amazingly kept filming and then handed Walter the unexposed film from the magazine. Walter immediately tore the film to pieces. Unfortunately, as she drove into the compound where the brothel was situated, our friend Chris had got in such a state that she had managed to hit the only other car within about a hundred and fifty miles. This was the middle of the desert! We all rushed out with the equipment but there was no car to be seen anywhere as by this time it was embedded in sand. Fortunately, by this time Walter had calmed down. He went crazy again, however, when the film was about to come out and threatened to sue, but then he had a heart attack and died, so that was the end of that. The freaky thing about the desert where we filmed is, on the one hand, you have a real sense of space and can scream and shout, but on the other, there is only one road in and one road out so your chances of escape are fairly remote unless you want to take to the hills. I can understand people getting claustrophobic there. I actually love Nevada, but it was full of strange people.

It's beautifully shot, with a real sense of space in which you punctuate life inside the ranch with shots of the moon rising and rather beautiful desert vistas.

86

The desert is a magnificent place and it's kind of pathetic that the best Walter could erect in its honour were these lousy little trailer homes. I suppose that all he wanted was money, but we were in the middle of this stunning landscape and stuck in this rather diminished compound with a fence around it. At night the moon and the stars were striking.

And were the hordes of visiting businessmen similarly unimpressed? We see a group of Japanese businessmen arrive and they don't seem exactly ecstatic to be there.
They had to sit on these couches covered in plastic and when you sat on them they made this awful noise as they let all the air out. It's modern, tacky Americana. There is obviously some great architecture in America but most of business America is just modern, pre-fabricated homes that are constructed anywhere and have nothing to do with their environment. I found that interesting and one of the most disappointing aspects about America; its architecture has got nothing to do with its place and the chicken ranch was a perfect embodiment of this and the pure profit motive.

Like a lot of your work, the film deals with those who form an underbelly of a society and are then in turn exploited in some way.
I wanted to make it more about this weird sorority house as opposed to a film about women being abused. I think that the women had come

The line up, *Chicken Ranch*

87

from very abusive backgrounds and the funny thing was that when it was transmitted in England the switchboards were blocked by people phoning to find out how they might get employment at the chicken ranch! I think that what we forget is that so many people have terrible lives that, compared to the lives of people in certain places, the chicken ranch really might not have appeared so bad. It was something of a safe haven and it was also by far the least depressing of the many places that we visited. Many of the places we looked at to film in were invariably just three girls and a mangy, ferocious dog in a smelly, really awful building. I felt that filming in that kind of ranch would just be an awful, depressing statement so there would be no point in making it. I wanted, in a sense, to see what the girls were like, how they functioned and related to each other and give a perspective on how they saw their world and their lives.

The sexual politics of the women are interesting and, in some way, they have a strong sense of self. They readily admit that they are prostitutes but they won't stand for any abuse from men and collectively rally round when one guy, Buck, becomes verbally abusive after failing to agree upon a discount rate.

There is a sense of empowerment and this is one of the things that I really wanted to come from the film. They were a really nice group of people, especially Fran. Through various circumstances, they had all ended up doing what they were doing but they still deserved respect and to be treated properly. They also deserved to be listened to; they all had a story that was worth telling. A lot of people just dismissed them as a bunch of hookers, but they were all so different from each other. I think of them as Linda, Connie, Becky and Kim. Kim was especially astute and had been to college and had a plan. There was a mixture of the brilliant and the tragic, such as Ginger, who was related to Wild Bill Hickock, and JJ, who had a bit of a drugs problem and was slightly out of control. I'm convinced that under different circumstances Ginger could have really made something of herself and used her wackiness in a constructive way.

The film is quite chaste, but there is the moment where you see the negotiation process between Mandy and a truck driver. This really cuts to the essence of the relationships between sex, money and power. It's also a very potent illustration of a working girl's life.

I was really surprised that we were allowed to film that far. Before, we had only ever got to film up to the moment where they entered the bedroom. This was also the only time that we were allowed to film the negotiation. A lot of the girls had a strong sense of propriety and didn't want us to film what happened in the bedroom. I think that inside the bedroom represented the moment where the women were in control and so was their moment. It was also a private moment. You certainly do see a hardness come out in Mandy and she makes it very clear that she's taking no shit. Before this moment she had been like a bubbly little girl. I remember the editor of the film, Julian Ware, was reluctant to put this scene in because he really liked Mandy and didn't want to reveal the tough aspect of her nature, which an audience would perhaps not find sympathetic, but I think that those contradictions are important.

Did you ever sit in the love chair? It looked a little imposing.
Actually I think that somebody had fallen off it only the week before. And when we were there the contraption looked somewhat precarious. I like it when Claudia says, 'I haven't mastered all the positions.'

There's a lot of humour in this film. I again refer to the Japanese tourists who don't speak a word of English. Conversely, there's also a real sadness and melancholy to it. Is this another aspect of your search for contradictions?
I think those places are very melancholic. I remember Pennebaker commenting that he would have installed a piano in there and had a guy playing honky-tonk piano in a New Orleans style. Maybe in the New Orleans brothels there is more romanticism, but *Chicken Ranch* offered a very accurate portrait of what it felt like there. Obviously, filming things does change the situation and, if anything, Sandi and I made the situation a little warmer by bringing more of a sense of community. Ordinarily the girls would remain much more isolated and not talk to each other so much; I think that one of the things that film always does is to encourage people to talk more about their lives and to be more extrovert.

Did the women in the film get to see it eventually?
They did. We had a lunatic screening in Caesar's Palace. I brought the film back and invited everybody to come. We also had a really nutty wrap party and I think that every hooker and every pimp in Las Vegas

put in an appearance. There were mounds of coke on top of all the tables and the party got completely out of control. I remember security tracking me down to tell me that they were unable to control the guests and so were going to have to ask them to leave. There were people prancing naked in the fountains and, of course, accosting visitors to the hotel in the lift. I retreated into the loo, where there was a phone, and called all the friends that I hadn't spoken to in months.

I remember the reaction to the film being a pretty positive one. I certainly don't remember anyone saying anything terrible. A couple of the girls had moved on in life. One of them had become an IBM programmer and was concerned about how the film was going to impact upon her future.

Apart from the calls enquiring as to how to join the chicken ranch, what other reaction did the film arouse when it was broadcast? For example, did it lead to an increased awareness of the lives of those living on the margins of society?
Prostitution and pornography generate in excess of something like $7 billion per year. Both are gigantic industries across the world. Often both are a form of slavery. I'm not sure that this was the case with the chicken ranch but you do get some sense of this with girls like JJ, who want to leave and begin a new life, and, regrettably, you know that they are never going to. It's labelled 'easy money' but you really have to work for it. There are not that many jobs out there for people with very little educational attainment and the overriding sense is, if the girls do leave, what are they going to do? There are a few minimum-wage jobs but this is pretty much all they can do.

Was it a difficult film to edit?
It was constructed around certain stories, such as the story of Connie, the girl who wasn't being picked. A lot of the girls had relationships with each other, such as Connie and Linda, so we tried to edit around those relationships whilst at the same time getting a portrait of the place and how it operated. In this way, it followed on from *Soldier Girls* in that the structure centred on the development of particular characters and individuals. We didn't have the same roll call of characters at the beginning, but we could have done, with people like Connie, JJ, Linda, Mandy, Fran and Walter.

From Chicken Ranch, *then, to a film tracing the development of American comedienne Lily Tomlin's show* The Search for Intelligent Life in the Universe *as it goes from rehearsal stage to huge Broadway success.*

How did the Lily Tomlin film come about?
Elsie Giorgi, a doctor who was Joan's mother's best friend, as well as being a doctor to the stars, suggested it. It all sounded like a great idea at the time but was just an absolute disaster from the very beginning. Lily Tomlin was very insecure about *The Search for Intelligent Life in the Universe*, the show she was researching, and was very reluctant to share her thoughts and feelings about it or involve us in the creative process. Peggy Feury, Lily's acting coach and a prominent member of the Lee Strasberg acting school, was fantastic. Peggy was killed in a car accident during the making of the film; she suffered from narcolepsy and fell asleep at the wheel. Our assistant John Kaufer also died. The irony was that here was this show, which I found interminable and never thought was very good, and all these real-life tragedies were happening around it that were not within the structure of the film. This is why I feel the film to be such a failure because it doesn't reveal our true experience of making it. I think there was a much more intelligent and all-embracing film to be made about the process of making it.

Did you enter into it with trepidation? I understand that Joan Churchill was a Tomlin fan and was the one who really wanted to do it.
I did it partly because Joan wanted to do it and because Lily Tomlin was a popular comedienne and I wanted to do something funny. But I didn't actually find Lily Tomlin funny. She could be funny when she was spontaneous, but she believed that spontaneity was a lower form of humour and that true humour had to be scripted and worked on. She was so uptight; everything was so contrived and measured.

At what point did you realize that making the film was going to become the stuff of nightmares?
We willed ourselves into believing that things would get better when the show got better and Lily got more confident. We would hang out in the Los Padres motel in San Diego, sometimes filming her for no more than half an hour a week, mindlessly doing nothing, listening to late-night shows and doing stomach crunches. I remember getting very

The search for intelligent life in the universe,
Lily Tomlin

itchy and so I went to see Elsie Giorgi, the doctor who had originally put us in touch with Lily Tomlin, and I said that I couldn't stop scratching myself. Elsie told me that I was under extreme stress and that the film was getting to me. I told Elsie that I didn't think that the film was getting to me; I was just so itchy, so itchy that I couldn't go out for dinner with people as I simply couldn't sit still. I was also getting these awful track marks. I took some pills which really knocked me out, but the itching still got worse and worse and, finally, I went to another doctor behind Elsie's back who told me that I had picked up scabies at the motel. I was so pleased to know that I hadn't lost my mind and didn't have to carry on taking those awful drugs. In short, my biggest memory of the film was having scabies and the loneliness of the motel.

And Lily was uncooperative during the making of the film?
She was an insecure, neurotic artist. I don't think that we necessarily

helped the situation. She was a control freak and I remember once going to her house and accidentally pushing a button on her filing cabinet locking all her papers, including all the papers for the show, inside. Lily didn't have a key for the cabinet but wouldn't trust any locksmith to open it, so we had to fly the one locksmith she trusted from San Francisco to her house – W. C. Fields's old place, by the way – who then fixed the lock and flew back to San Francisco. We had to pay for all this.

On another occasion, I was in this enormous Cadillac that we were using as a crew car. Lily had these huge electric Spanish bastion gates and, because the car was so long and we were driving in quite slowly, the gates closed on the car and had an electrical burnout. The car was wedged in the gates for three days, during which time Lily couldn't drive in or out. She absolutely hated me by the end, a situation not helped by the fact that I believe in answering back. So she would say something to me and I would answer back, which she saw as some kind of impertinence as opposed to having a conversation. She would say to Sheryl, her big butch assistant, 'Sheryl, did he say that to me? Well, you tell him . . .' and I would say, 'Lily, I'm still here, why don't you tell me yourself?' At which point she would start hyperventilating. We should have filmed these scenes because she was just so unreasonable and so out of touch with the world. I thought that she and Jane Wagner had a very interesting creative relationship. It was also a sexual relationship, but Tomlin wouldn't accept that she was gay then so we couldn't allude to this fact and we all had to live this lie regarding their relationship. We became part of this mad circus that went on for almost a year and a half.

Was that how long the film lasted?
Yes! Lily kept postponing the date on which the show was going to open on Broadway. I wanted to change tack and make a more critical film, and this was the source of my first disagreement with Joan. Joan felt a loyalty towards Lily because of Elsie Giorgi, but I was dying to get up to a few tricks and to fudge the boundaries of the film to show what a monster Lily was.

And Tomlin was equally, if not more, difficult once it was finished.
The show was a Broadway success, and at this point Lily decided that we were going to benefit from this success and she was going to sue us

because she felt that we had exceeded the amount of performance footage that we were entitled to under the contract. HBO wanted to buy our film, Lily wanted to sell her own film, another making of the show, to HBO and didn't want us to compete, so this awful lawsuit started up.

Did Joan's attitude to Lily waver once the lawsuits started flying?
Joan is a tremendously loyal person and, despite everything, had great respect for Lily. I have no respect for Lily at all. Of all the people I have filmed, she and Courtney Love are pretty close to the bottom of the totem pole. Both are prima donnas and both seem to be frightened of being even vaguely truthful. There is a pretence that one is supposed to accept in a very unquestioning way and I simply won't be bullied like that. The irony of it is that we went into it with the intention of making a very positive film about Lily, and I think if she had trusted us and been more open then that is what would have happened. Instead of that, it turned into the worst experience that I've ever had, not only with the day-to-day filming – which was utterly miserable – but the end product too was not worthy of her or us. It also took far longer than any other film I have done.

What was the outcome of Tomlin's lawsuit?
It taught me a lot about entertainment law. We actually did draw up a contract with Lily specifying how much rehearsal and how much Broadway show we could include, but as with so many contracts it was open to dispute. In fact, we used Fred Wiseman's lawyer Bud Mandelstan. Then, when the lawsuit happened, Lily Tomlin sued us for $7.2 million and managed to get a restraining order to stop the film coming out. This obviously screwed up all our distribution possibilities. One always has to remember that the threat of a lawsuit is generally always enough to frighten most distributors away because, if they've invested money in an advertising campaign and the release is then put back, well, that money is more or less thrown away. So sometimes, even if there isn't a legitimate lawsuit, the mere threat of it will put distributors off. In this case, there was an actual restraining order, which was terrible. However, Joan and I decided to continue and hired our own lawyer, which was, of course, terribly expensive.

Lily Tomlin had a real heavyweight lawyer in Dan Sklar, whilst we had a lawyer named Shirley Hufstedler. I always remember speaking to Fred Wiseman's lawyer and asking if Shirley would be able to measure up, and he replied, 'Shirley Hufstedler is such a heavyweight that Dan Sklar won't be able to hold her sweatpants after the first round,' which is pretty much what happened. Shirley was formidable and had been the Secretary of Education in President Carter's cabinet. The restraining order was lifted and we were able to distribute the film, but Lily Tomlin had a lot more money than us so we then came to a settlement that we would do the theatrical run of the film, it would have a PBS showing and it would go on Channel Four, but that we wouldn't be able to sell it to HBO and we wouldn't be able to sell it elsewhere. This is pretty much where things still are, though I hear from Joan that Lily Tomlin has had a change of mind about it.

Joan actually took on the job of distributing the film across the US and put up a good show, with the film playing in something like seventy cities. It was a full-time job and I remember she got really ill, developing a cyst in her stomach. It was terribly stressful. By this time I had, of course, run off back to England, having had quite enough of the whole thing. It was such a bad experience and has given me the unfair reputation of attracting lawsuits. If you have seen the film, you'd see that there is clearly nothing worthy of a lawsuit in it; the whole thing was more to do with greed because Lily simply saw our film as competition to the sale of her own film to HBO.

I have to say that it doesn't feel like a Nick Broomfield film. It's almost as if you have been gagged.
I was severely gagged. I felt really restricted creatively; I didn't find the show funny and was forced to defer my feelings about Lily Tomlin's humour. This was a fatal mistake because if you don't find something funny then you have to assume that other people are also not going to find it funny. It was, however, a really useful learning curve, and I think that you can learn from things that go seriously wrong and are painful just as much as you can learn from things that go right.

There are a few very telling moments that hint at the situation in which you were working and the kind of film you perhaps could have made. One is where Sheryl has to ring Lily up in her motel room and tell her about the imperfections with the poster, and Lily obviously hangs up on her. Another is where Sheryl relaxes a bit and starts to talk about drug experiences. Lily becomes concerned that she is a drug addict and threatens to fire her.

Sheryl had to put up with a lot of crap. There seemed to be some sort of weird sexual dynamic going on. The situation was very unsatisfactory and, more than anything, hypocritical. You kind of hope that a great artist can just be who they are, so I found this very disappointing. She was supposed to be some kind of heroine, which was why Joan wanted to do the film.

Though the show was a massive success, when Tomlin invites audience feedback during the rehearsal process there are dissenting voices.
Tomlin felt that there was too much lesbian humour in the piece, and Sheryl and the women working on the show just couldn't understand this reaction. Their attitude was, 'Everybody knows that you're gay, so why not be proud of who you are?' It's very disingenuous. Lily's relationship with Jane Wagner was at the core of her creativity and at the core of her humour, and yet we were prevented from going there.

The Broadway star, like Lily Tomlin, rehearsing for a production has become something of a staple of the American documentary in recent years.[9]
Maybe other films work well, but *Lily Tomlin* sits like an uncooked dumpling in my stomach so, to tell you the truth, I haven't seen them. I did meet Elaine Stritch and I thought that she was an amazing character. I also think that her show was so much more honest than the Lily Tomlin one; I saw it in London when she was over here. I'm personally much more interested in films such as *Don't Look Back* (1967) or *Cocksucker Blues* (1972) or *Gimme Shelter* (1970). I guess I prefer rock and roll to the Broadway stuff.

The film marks something of a transition period in your work in that for your next film, Driving Me Crazy, *you actually film the disintegration of the film that you are making. It also marks a burgeoning interest in the notion of celebrity and celebrity figures.*
I'm not sure that I would use the word 'celebrity', but I certainly became more interested in iconic figures such as Eugene Terre'Blanche, Chicco Twala, Heidi Fleiss, etc. I certainly went in a different direction, but I think that this stemmed more from *Driving Me Crazy*. I wanted to make a more commercial film that might reach a wider audience and I think the icons were, in a sense, the maguffin; they were the ostensible subject but they weren't really what the film was about.

Take *Heidi Fleiss*, for example; I mean Heidi Fleiss is in it, but it's actually about much wider things. It became something of a commercial calling card.

Driving Me Crazy *was the first film in which Broomfield appeared significantly and was a major change in style for the director as he became the axis on which the 'story' spins. Ostensibly hired to make an experimental film with elements of fiction involving a documentary film-maker following the transition of an ambitious new musical –* Body and Soul *– from rehearsals to stage success, Broomfield instead documents the ensuing chaos and personal crises as the film, and the production, lurches from one disaster to the next.*

Driving Me Crazy *has probably set the template for your subsequent career and the style for which you are most commonly known.*
To a certain extent you are always reacting to your last film – emotionally at least – and *Lily Tomlin*, as we discussed, was much less than the experience of making it. I found myself emerging with a fount of after-dinner stories that sadly weren't in the film and the feeling that these stories should have been the film and that the film should have been in the dustbin. This is not a great feeling. I was also really broke as we were embroiled in a lengthy lawsuit and had no residuals as we were precluded from doing so. I was desperate to make some money and was called out of the blue by Andrew Braunsberg and asked if I wanted to make a film about a musical titled *Body and Soul*. I met Andrew, who had seen and loved *Soldier Girls*. He had a lovely wife, Gabrielle, who was very keen on Andrew and I doing something because she saw me as somebody who was, in a way, quite youthful and fun. Andrew had previously worked with Roman Polanski and Paul Morrissey, and I think Gabrielle wanted her husband to hook up with someone who looked fairly clean-living. In other words, Gabrielle got me the job. I then met André Heller, the showbiz impresario behind the show in Vienna and again later in New York, where the rehearsals were taking place before the show transferred to Munich. When I got there Gabrielle wasn't around and Andrew was installed in the most expensive hotel in New York. Andrew is known as 'old silver tongue' because he is very charming and can quite literally talk people into doing anything. André Heller is known as 'frenzy' to his friends. He's a very astute man and incredibly rich and successful, hence his enormous art collection. There was a lot

Body and Soul, *Driving me Crazy*

of disagreement about the financing of the film; Virgin Telemünchen and another television station were involved and there was an enormous amount of disagreement regarding what kind of film this was going to be. Heller and Braunsberg had this idea that it was going to be like a real-life *Fame* but with one vital extra ingredient: certain parts of the film were going to be entirely scripted. The writer, Joe Hindy, also played the character that was writing the story. I don't know if it was a measure of my disbelief that this could work, but I never understood what the story was going to be.

Did you know going into the project that there would be this element or was this sprung upon you once you had already signed up?
Andrew kept going on about this aspect, which was originally going to be about a theatre producer called Max, and I kept explaining that I didn't understand it, but Andrew told me not to worry and that it would all become clear once I got to New York. There were never any actual pages, although at one point Joe Hindy claimed to have written the pages but had never been paid. I just didn't understand how you could film the development of the show and the various characters within the show and then have a completely separate fictional element as well. Anyway, during one of the meetings I could hear Andrew arguing with the various financiers and the original agreed budget of $1.3 million was then cut to about $300,000. I got a sniff that things

The irrepressible André Heller, the man behind *Body and Soul*

were about to go very badly wrong and after *Lily Tomlin* I didn't want
the same experience again, so I told Andrew about my reservations
concerning the budget and the structure of the film and explained that
I was going to fly back to LA and that he should let me know when
things were resolved. Andrew's reaction was, 'Look, we at least have
all this money, we are staying in the best hotel in New York, so why
don't we just make an experimental film? How often will you get the
chance to blow all this money? Think of it as a really well-financed
student film.' I told Andrew that I would sleep on it and that we would
talk again in the morning because things were fraught and frenzied. As
I stayed up all night pondering, I remembered Michael Rubbo's
Waiting for Fidel (1974) and Ross McElwee's *Sherman's March*
(1986), both of which are absolutely brilliant, and I thought that
maybe I could make a film about not just the show and the development of the show, but about all the disagreements and the characters
and the disputes between the financiers during the making of the film.
I also wondered what the fuck could I do with Joe Hindy? Perhaps

chuck him in as another ingredient and so roll back the boundaries of the film. My dilemma, my search for what the story was, would of course be in there too.

As I started making it, I realized that I should use a voice-over and so I got hold of copies of *Sherman's March* and *Waiting for Fidel* and watched them very carefully, thinking, well, if they can do it then maybe I can too. At the back of my mind, however, was Derek Malcolm's comment about my voice. Like anyone I had doubts, but it was such a desperate situation that I felt I had to go for it. As I started to make it – and even though it was extremely fraught and crazy – I was amusing myself because I thought, well, I can just put all this in, and I was beginning to really have fun with the form and playing with it for once. I had always felt somewhat subservient to form, so making *Driving Me Crazy* was quite liberating. I was, of course, worried that the film would be a piece of shit, but it was incredible fun, the gods seemed to be with me and I felt that this was the only way to tell an incredibly complicated story that, in essence, was an absolute mess.

There is a perception that you are slightly buffoonish and antagonistic in the film. Is this a deliberate attempt to draw a reaction from people? For example, in Driving Me Crazy *you manage to blow all the lights during rehearsals. Assistant show director Howard Porter spends the entire film on the cusp of killing you.*
It was tense anyway. Howard is a bit of a prima donna and the next minute he would really love you. I think they all really liked me! There was also an incident where I accidentally managed to hit choreographer George Faison on the head with an ice cube, but it was this moment that probably persuaded George and Howard to do the film. George and Howard loved being on camera and were anarchists, so they loved the anarchy of the film and the uncertain spirit in which it was being made. I think there was an element of people feeling used because what André Heller most enjoyed was seeing all those shows and all the rehearsals because it was like having his own Apollo theatre. In reality, all the rappers and the roller skaters had no place in the show, but because he was a stager of spectaculars this is what he really loved. Heller would arrange all these call backs, we would film them and then Heller would just fuck off leaving chaos everywhere. What happened was that we got blamed for leading the performers to believe that they were actually going to be in the show. I do think that on

Fiery but fun, Howard Porter,
Driving me Crazy

occasion we made things worse – for example, the lighting disaster –
but in our defence it was a very big room and we actually did have a
very experienced gaffer, even if the actual lighting crew was somewhat
gung-ho and able to seemingly blow up and short-circuit entire buildings. There was, however, a cowboy feeling to the film production that
I as director had to assume responsibility for, and if you hire people
then it does also become your responsibility to fire them too if they
don't perform correctly.

And were you forced to fire people?
We did lose the original cameraman because I felt that a lot of us were
propping him up. Nick Doob is actually a very good cameraman who
had worked a lot with Pennebaker,[10] but he was used to working in a
far more *cinema vérité* way and didn't really fully grasp the kind of
film we were making. Make no mistake though, Nick is a lovely guy
and very talented but I didn't feel that he was doing his best work with
us. That said, left to my own devices I wouldn't have dismissed him,

but after a screening at DuArt Andrew Braunsberg encouraged me to do so.

The cameraperson did seem to get very good at hitting Mercedes Ellington on the head.
I'm not sure that was Nick Doob. In fact, I'm sure it wasn't. But yes, this did become a problem.

The impression I always had of this film was that you happened upon a structure to salvage a nightmare, but it's now apparent to me that this wasn't the case at all as your approach was entirely premeditated and intentional.
It was a nightmare from the beginning, especially in regard to the financing, but I just decided to make this a virtue of the kind of film I could make. At the beginning of every film you start to scope out your conceptual approach and make decisions as to what style, form and tone you are going to incorporate.

The tone here is very comic. There is particularly good use of reaction shots and the voice-over is hilarious, especially after one particularly disastrous encounter with Joe Hindy when you exclaim, 'It was at this point that I began to have grave reservations about the project.'
That moment is the essence of the film. Sometimes you are thrown things that are so wacky, and the fact that they don't gel becomes what makes the film. We all work differently but, for me, making these films is about working with what you have and working with the problems. OK, you start off making a film about Margaret Thatcher but in the end it turns into this, this and this, and, in a way, that defines the subject. Everyone would love to have an easy film and I always admire those BBC crews who have a schedule. They know that in one week's time at two o'clock they'll be meeting so and so and then they send the crew along for pre-lighting, but I've never ever had that kind of experience. It's generally me pursuing people who don't want to be in the film or door-stepping them. If someone agrees to be filmed by me, I invariably have to be in the car and outside their door before they can change their mind. That's my experience and that partly explains the selection of subjects.

I have chosen subjects that are very off-limits; the reason that people hadn't made a film about Kurt Cobain or Courtney Love before is that they are fucking hard to do. Nobody wants to talk to you, they largely

Choreographer Mercedes Ellington just prior to being hit on the
head with a boom mic, *Driving me Crazy*

feature characters who duck and dive, and you have to come up with a
style and a form that will encompass that and embrace it to enable you
to get a story out of it, come what may. It's exciting in a way because you
can do stories that are impossible with traditional methods; you're flying
by the seat of your pants. For people that don't have that kind of experience, it is difficult to appreciate how tough these films are to make.

There are a couple of moments in Driving Me Crazy *when it does all
look like it is about to spiral out of control. You get very angry when
viewing the rushes with Herbert Rimbach, one of the German producers, who criticizes everything you have shot and deems it unusable.*
There were several moments like this in the film where it was out of
my control, and these largely revolved around the occasions when it
looked as if the film was going to be cancelled. There were numerous
reasons for this, partly because we had outworn our welcome, partly
because what we had shot was considered unusable and then because
the financing was going to be completely cut off. Such moments were
very disheartening because we had invested so much energy and time
into it and I was convinced that we had something great there. I am

also one of those people who, when I start something, have to finish it. There's only one film I haven't finished in all the years I have been making films and that was a project set in a tax office that I was making for Thames Television.

Why was that not finished?
It would have been, apart from the fact that I had a union crew who were just impossible. I feel that sometimes your most interesting ideas and discoveries happen when you are really up against it, so you just have to promise yourself to follow it through to its conclusion. When you are making a film there are many times each and every day when you wished that you weren't doing it, but with *Driving Me Crazy* I was also convinced that there was something really interesting about it and that it was also something that I could learn from. It continued to be a nightmare right up until the end. After we had cut it, there was a terrible problem with the music rights, which I ended up having to clear, and it was very expensive and difficult to trace all the composers and to then secure the rights. John Mister, the editor on the film, was thankfully fantastic at doing that and had a lot of music training and was a real trooper in getting all that done.

To top it all, Andrew Braunsberg, who was the producer of the film, refused to sign a release form giving us permission to use his own image in the film. I remember that there was a very amusing incident in the editing room, and I wish I had filmed this: Mike Watts from Virgin, who had sunk a lot of money into the film too, was there and Andrew, who had by this time taken up fencing, arrived in full fencing gear. He literally was swatting Mike Watts off and then made a run for the taxi having not signed the release form. He simply refused to be in the film, meaning that we were going to have to cut him out. Fortunately, Gabrielle again came to the rescue and forced Andrew to sign. Gabrielle was such a great sport. She said, 'Andrew, just sign it, it's not like any of it is untrue.'

Let's talk about the relationship with Joe Hindy. Much of the humour, intentional or otherwise, revolves around him.
We were wicked to him really, but he did take himself terribly seriously.

Did you deliberately provoke him?
We did, especially in the scene when he was doing his acted scene. It

was too much of a temptation not to. I refused to film the scene seriously because it was just such an appalling scene. I did have a really crazy cameraman, Rob Levi, who took the bait when I asked him to go in on Joe as fast as possible. Of course, he couldn't stop and went crashing into him. By this point Joe's sense of humour had given in and he just couldn't stand it any more.

There's a sequence with Joe where you take him to shoot in Harlem and a young black woman talks about the mayor's plans to move the blacks out and gentrify Harlem. You also, as well as pricking the egocentric nature of show business, show how the black performers are frequently reduced to racial stereotypes.
I wanted to show how there was a dream that there would be an opportunity for the black performers and for many of them that dream would fade; that's what traditionally happens. Alongside sport, show business has traditionally offered one of their few exits from poverty. This sadly hasn't shifted that much in the US. As for the gentrification of Harlem, well, that had already started to happen, and it still continues today. I wanted to take a look at how there are areas that are clearly marked along racial lines – something that I look at in greater detail in *Biggie and Tupac*, alongside notions of black justice and white justice. It's frankly impossible to look at anything in America without coming across that racial divide.
    It's also interesting that, although André Heller loved a lot of the black rappers and the body poppers, he knew that these performers would not go down well with a production that would play to very conservative Germans when it opened in Munich and then toured throughout Austria.

You end up having a meeting with Andrew in a broom cupboard.
This was a real moment of despair when we were all a bit worried and there was a definite feeling that the ship was going down; we were the orchestra that were still playing and, like them, it didn't look like we were going to get paid. Just about everyone was owed money.

There is also quite a tense telephone conversation with Andrew in which you enquire about your own salary. Accompanying the conversation is a quite beautiful panning shot of Manhattan. Why this juxtaposition?
It was cameraman Rob Levi's idea of doing the Manhattan shot; I

wasn't even there when he did it. It was a summation of the situation in Manhattan. It was the last thing we shot before going on to Munich, but as it looked like the financiers were about to close the film, it may also have been the last shot of the film. We were also having to act in a very undignified manner and scramble around for what was owed us. It was rats off a sinking ship at that point. I also thought that this elegant and beautiful shot of the Manhattan skyline offered a nice contrast.

When you do get to Munich, you are only allowed to film three minutes of Body and Soul, *but it was a massive success there. Did this leave all those who had been involved with the film with a sensation of celebration?*
Andrew enjoys telling people, rather amusingly, that it was the most successful theatrical production in Germany since the Second World War. I'm not sure about the feeling of celebration. I thought that it was pretty kitschy and actually a pretty bad show. I was also disappointed because it just perpetuated racial stereotypes and I'd hoped that it would be something more. The choreographers were also disappointed that it wasn't more contemporary.

You did seem rather taken with André's assistant, Michaela May.
She may have also been one of the ingredients in my decision to make the film. I remember first seeing Michaela walking into the room, and it took a while for my mind to catch up with my eyes. I was also interested in her because my mother is from Prague and, even though Michaela was German, I connected her and her exoticism with that part of Europe. I didn't put so much of this in the film, but it's also fascinating to consider André's infatuation with her. André is Jewish and Michaela, a former dancer, was the daughter of a shoemaker who then went off to join the SS. She was an irrepressible flirt, but I did find her to be a great source of energy and inspiration when making it. When I make a film I frequently find a character that I am attracted to – and not necessarily just in a physical manner – someone who I can look forward to seeing each day when the filming is heavy going, and Michaela was certainly that. It was also interesting to publicly acknowledge her in this way.

Do you think Driving Me Crazy *took your career to a new level? It played to large audiences worldwide.*

The flirtatious Michaela,
Driving me Crazy

I think so. It certainly presented a way forward. It's a very important film for me in terms of taking a risk and it working, feeling free to put in your wilder thoughts – thoughts that would normally remain private – and treating film as something that you can play with. You can be over-cautious about what people will say and think about you and your film, and I firmly believe that film-making and personal development are all about taking risks. You have to trust yourself and not be ashamed of who you are.

What was the reaction of your contemporaries to seeing the film?
I remember Colin Young saying that he would have been proud to have made it, and that for me was the greatest possible accolade. It's funny because I've never really talked to Pennebaker or Chris Hegedus in great detail about my work. I know that David Maysles hates my work and is also critical of the films of Michael Moore and Ross McElwee. Richard Leacock is more experimental and open in some ways, in comparison to some of the others, and I think appreciates my work. He certainly appreciates McElwee as he was one of his teachers.

With many of these people you will talk about the problems you may be having with a particular film, but that rarely extends to another conversation about the finished work and the extent to which one loves or loathes it.

Do you see its influence on the films that were made subsequently?
I think it was an important foundation film in terms of moving a certain form of storytelling on. People have called it post-modernist and I feel that it is a little like those early Tom Wolfe pieces in that the getting of the interview and the circumstances of the interview are every bit as important as the interview itself. I do think that *Driving Me Crazy* did mark a big step forward in writing, film-making and in our understanding of how subjects are treated. It broke certain boundaries and let the audience in at an earlier part in the stories.

And what did Joan Churchill, who you were no longer working with at this point, make of your 'new direction' – to quote Spinal Tap?
Joan was very supportive. She was initially suspicious and wary of the style, and I think that it has certainly worked better in some films than in others. The subject is what is important and should not be subservient to the style. Joan and I next worked together on *Juvenile Liaison 2*, a slightly difficult film because we were no longer living together at the time, but to have made *Juvenile Liaison 2* in the same style as *Driving Me Crazy* would have been pointless. There I was just something to hold things together and connect the strands of the people I had interviewed before.

The last word should go to Joe Hindy. He did give you the title for the film.
'You are driving me crazy.' I also love the line from Andrew Braunsberg when he informs me that my 'charm has run out'. There are some great lines in there. Of course, Joe also says, 'You are talking about doing a feature film. Your actors will hang you.' Well, he was right about that. Those words certainly echoed around my brain when making *Diamond Skulls*.

'*You are Driving me Crazy!*', Joe Hindy loses his cool

Notes

1. Directed by Peter Watkins, *Punishment Park* is a pseudo-documentary in which political dissenters can choose federal prison or endure the three-day ordeal of the futuristic Punishment Park.
2. Gunnery Sgt. Hartman.
3. On Friday 30 April, photographs of US soldiers abusing Iraqi prisoners appeared in various newspapers across the globe, prompting universal condemnation. The pictures showed US troops smiling and giving the thumbs-up signal as they posed with naked Iraqi soldiers posed to simulate sex acts. It later transpired, however, that a number of the photos were fake, the decision to publish them ultimately costing *Daily Mirror* editor Piers Morgan his job.
4. David and Albert, whose films include *Gimme Shelter* (1970) and *Grey Gardens* (1975).

5. Amanda Spake is the editor of feminist publication *Mother Jones*. The quote is reproduced on www.nickbroomfield.com.

6. The director of counter-culture classic *Medium Cool*, Haskell Wexler's filmography as a cinematographer includes: *The Thomas Crown Affair* (1968), *One Flew Over the Cuckoo's Nest* (1975), *Matewan* (1987) and *Mulholland Falls* (1996).

7. A regular collaborator with Ken Loach and Stephen Frears, Chris Menges' CV also includes: *Local Hero* (1983), *The Killing Fields* (1984) and *Michael Collins* (1996).

8. Following the success of Nicolas Philibert's *Être et avoir*, the schoolteacher at the centre of the film subsequently attempted to negotiate with the film-makers for a cut of the film's profits.

9. One such example is *Moon Over Broadway* (1997), D. A. Pennebaker's and Chris Hegedus's documentary about Carol Burnett.

10. Nick Doob's credits with D. A. Pennebaker include: *Monterey Pop* (1968), *Ziggy Stardust and the Spiders from Mars* (1973), *The War Room* (1993) and *Only the Strong Survive* (2002).

4

Close Shaves

Diamond Skulls, The Leader, His Driver and the Driver's Wife, Monster in a Box, Too White for Me

Gabriel Byrne and Amanda Donohue,
Diamond Skulls, Nick's fiction debut

Broomfield's – thus far – sole foray into fiction film-making, Diamond Skulls *revolves around a group of young British guardsmen (led by Hugo, played by Gabriel Byrne, who is embroiled in a passionate if insanely jealous marriage to Amanda Donohue's Ginny) who are forced to group together to cover up a hit-and-run incident that occurred at the end of a night of drunken revelry.*

JW: *Why did you make the decision to move into fiction film-making?*
NB: Originally I wanted to do a film on Lord Lucan; I think that my documentary side was interested in the reality and facts of his story and the nitty-gritty of that very male world. I was intrigued by the details of somebody like Lord Lucan, who had identical shoes, shirts and suits and who was part of that male club that is so uneasy around women. I'm probably stating all this much clearer here than I did at the time because what happened was the writer, Tim Rose Price, felt that as the children of Lord Lucan were still alive it would be disrespectful to them to do something that would be about their father and was uncomfortable doing that story. With hindsight, which is always useless, I should have just maintained that this was the story that I wanted to tell, accepted Tim's very valid reason for not wanting to tell it, but parted ways and found myself another writer.

What happened from here on in was that the story we came up with lost its direction because it had nothing to do with the story that I was originally interested in. I wasn't interested in doing something along the lines of a comedy involving Ian Carmichael and Sir Michael Hordern, who are both brilliant actors. Once I'd lost telling the Lucan story and had fallen in love with the allure of Amanda Donohue, I was much more interested in making an erotic film involving her and Gabriel Byrne that was of a whole other nature. The only trouble was that the script didn't reflect this, and my life up until this point as a documentarian had always been about learning how to incorporate the film and your ideas together in a spontaneous way and, where appropriate, changing things. This is less possible when you are making a feature film and have a large crew. The script is used as the bible from which everyone is working, and when you try and change things you make a lot of people unhappy.

'What can I say? A great cast, producer, writer and cinematographer ... But I think I kind of screwed it up.'[1] Is this still how you feel?
I still don't think that I've entirely recovered from the pain of it because I haven't replaced it with a better film. It's a whole different way of telling a story and what I've always been good at is working with what there is and the instinct of the occasion. If I do make another fiction film, which is something I am thinking about doing now, it will be closely modelled on reality and it will be with a very small crew and much less structured than *Diamond Skulls* was. Even the title is something that I hate, and I never did really like it. It was called *Dark Obsession* in the States, which while not the greatest title is slightly better. Apparently, it actually made a fair amount of money in the US – several million – but really it's just a mess.

How did you find the discipline of having to direct actors?
I loved directing and working with the actors, and I would consider Gabriel Byrne a good friend. I obviously had a very passionate relationship with Amanda, so I don't think there was a problem there; but it was more about not thinking it through properly in terms of marrying my approach to what the film was actually trying to say. It was neither one thing nor the other. As the director, it is your responsibility to get the script right; the director can't go round blaming other people. If you think that your script is not right then you shouldn't move on the film; unfortunately I did. I come back again to the importance of the structure and the execution. This was a different way of thinking and working for me. I am used to having the freedom to construct the film at the end of the shoot and, obviously, with a fiction piece this is more difficult to do. There is a way around this, I suppose, by allowing more room for improvisation . . .

Are there any aspects of the film that please you?
I think the sex scenes are the best things in it, and if it had been more a study of an obsessive sexual relationship then it would have been more interesting. This was also the most personal aspect of the film and that was probably what I brought to it. The rest of it just doesn't work.

Do you regret having made it?
I regret having made something that shouldn't have been made at the time it was made. If it had been about an obsessive sexual relationship that ended in a mess and had had that kind of energy running all the way through it, then it could have been a great film. But it wasn't about that; that was only a small part of it. Producer Colin Vaines said it rather well when he said that 'the film brought out the worst in you and the worst in Tim Rose Price'. It did. There was this uneasy marriage between a study of the upper class and a study of sexual obsession, and the two were different films.

The critics were very tough on the film.
Rightly so. I've only managed to watch it once and that was with an audience in Sweden where I felt safe. Even that was incredibly painful. I remember the first time I saw an assembly of the film in a screening room; I was more or less horizontal. By the end of it I couldn't believe that this was something that I'd had anything to do with. In a sense, it's the only film I feel this way about. I watched my Spalding Gray film *Monster in a Box* again the other day and was surprised by how much I liked it and what a good job I'd done and how well it worked. But this . . . It was a pity that *Diamond Skulls* worked out that way. A lot of it goes back to remembering why you are making the film, what it is that you want to say, where it's going and what your audience is and not really deviating from that. Once you deviate from it, that's potentially a big problem.

Well, I wish you luck with the next fiction picture.
Me too. I have certainly decided that I will do the next one in my style rather than trying to emulate Ridley Scott or somebody rather badly and looking like a doofus at the end of it. It will be more a question of capitalizing on what I am good at and forming the structure of the crew and the approach to the subject around that. I would certainly

simplify the whole process because with feature films there's this huge servicing arm. I really can't understand why an actor would need a car service. Why can't they get up in the morning and drive themselves to work like normal people have to? I also can't understand why they need dressers. It's as if they become subnormal and are unable to dress themselves.

Finally, I also hated being called 'Guv'nor' by all these people in the crew. I viewed it as a derogatory term. Film crews have a very rigid pecking order that is a lot like a micro-class system and I hated that. Some directors love it. It's like the idea of having your name on the back of a chair; I can't think of anything worse.

That's a pity. I was thinking of calling this book The Guv'nor.
Oh God . . . Of course, there are people like Ken Loach or Pawel Pawlikowski who work in a very different way and shoot no matter what. I am also a big fan of Bernard Rose's *Ivansxtc* (2000). On recollection, the other aspect that I found exasperating was that the camera suddenly became like this huge dinosaur, so a simple shot that you would have ordinarily got with a smaller camera suddenly required fifty people, the laying of tracks for the dolly and half a day's shoot. And then you might not even use it.

You returned to documentary with Juvenile Liaison 2. *Was it a welcome return?*
What I missed in doing *Diamond Skulls* was that feeling of being on the road, and I also got fed up with having to be responsible for the answers to so many peripheral questions, such as what did I want people to wear, where I wanted a bathtub positioned for a particular scene, and so on. Although I really enjoyed working with the actors and also enjoyed the actual shooting, I found the getting to the point of shooting exhausting. It was like every department had to make their presence known, just as the camera was about to start rolling, as if to prove that they are there and they are doing something and that they do deserve the exorbitant amounts of money they are being paid. Frequently, the costume designer would rush in and ruffle out a crinkle on a suit and then, without fail, the make-up artist would appear and start to powder somebody's nose or the props designer would remove a piece of lint from a teacup or something. I think that the majority of all that is irrelevant to an audience. If the audience is con-

centrating on these details, then as a film-maker you have ultimately failed. Maybe I needed to be more severe with my crew but I found that whole side of it awful, so I was delighted to get back to a tiny crew where you were juggling to fit in with what was happening rather than this juggernaut constantly bearing down upon you. *Juvenile Liaison 2* was also a good choice because I knew the subject well and so didn't regard the project as a huge creative challenge; I could also use it as a recovery process from making what was a really bad film in *Diamond Skulls*.

So you decided to go to South Africa to film The Leader, His Driver and the Driver's Wife?

Filmed in Ventersdorp, South Africa, The Leader, His Driver and the Driver's Wife *is a telling portrait of notorious right-wing AWB party leader Eugene Terre'Blanche and his frequently buffoonish, politically Neanderthal followers. The film is significant in that it showed Broomfield consistently pursuing and failing to get an interview with Terre'Blanche – who later uses every attempt to humiliate the director – in the end turning the leader's attempts to evade him into the under-pinning structure of the film.*

We'd actually gone to South Africa to make a different film. There were these Christian encounter groups operating in the townships, where a lot of black kids had never touched white skin. This is before Mandela came to power, whilst De Klerk was still in power and desperately hanging on. These groups were having these encounters between black and white kids in which they would talk to each other about their issues and then finally touch each other's skin; a lot of the black kids were convinced that if they touched a white person they would melt. But this was still under apartheid and the scheme was very limited and the encounter so measured and pathetic that when we got there it just wasn't a film worth making.

There is a sequence in The Leader, His Driver *where you do film black kids in a township reacting jubilantly to your presence and touching your skin. Was this a moment from the original film?*

One of the things that I remember from the first film was walking through the townships and kids touching our skin in amazement, so I was influenced by that and I think that it was a good initial introduction

Eugene Terre'Blanche turns on the charm,
The Leader, His Driver and the Driver's Wife

to South Africa. I was very frustrated by the church and its hypocrisy because it could have had very instructive encounters, but it just didn't know what to do with these reservoirs of emotion. I called Channel Four and told them that I didn't think there was a film here. Of course, it's always a mistake to do that without having a plan B. I was making the film with Barry Ackroyd and Riete Oord, and Riete, who is partly Dutch, spoke enough to understand what was going on. After I'd read a number of very good articles in the *Guardian* about Eugene Terre'Blanche we decided to drive to Ventersdorp. As soon as we saw it and Terre'Blanche, it was obvious that there was a great film there.

I called up Peter Moore and Channel Four with this new idea, and I remember Peter asking if it would be a good 'other' film. Peter then spoke to Riete and tried to get an assurance from her that I wouldn't be in it.

Why did he not want you to appear?
Because I'd only appeared in *Driving Me Crazy*. Once I'd made *The Leader, His Driver* and it was so successful, everyone always insisted that I was in the film whether I wanted to be or not. On *Fetishes*, for example, I saw no reason for me to be in the film, but HBO absolutely insisted. On *Aileen: The Life and Death of a Serial Killer* I really reduced my presence considerably to the bare minimum of being a witness and asking a few questions. With *The Leader, His Driver* it was an inherent part of the structure that I be in the film, and I couldn't think of any other way of doing it.

How did you secure the interview with Terre'Blanche?
Terre'Blanche had contempt for foreign journalists; he was a bully and a thug renowned for having a terrible temper. He is one of those people with a cloud of darkness around him. He didn't take us seriously because most journalists would come out from Johannesburg or Pretoria with a few questions, arrange an interview with him and then leave the same afternoon. That was what Terre'Blanche knew of journalism or documentary film-makers. It was how South African broadcasting worked. When we arrived in our rather shambolic VW and stayed for weeks he thought that we were just a bunch of film-student idiots who didn't know what we were doing. If there was another journalist in town he would always cancel us for this journalist because he regarded us as unimportant.

That's very funny because the thing that annoys him most when you do finally interview him is the possibility that you have been off interviewing someone more important than him.
Eugene Terre'Blanche came from a very military background. He was one of the main bodyguards for the Prime Minister Hendrik Frensch Verwoerd. He was obviously not that successful as Verwoerd was assassinated in 1966. Terre'Blanche came from that whole uptight Afrikaner background: heavy drinking, heavy meat eating and heavy womanizing. A bigot is really what he was, and highly unpleasant too.

119

He wrote poetry and went whoring, mainly with black whores. When they went to these training camps it was mainly an excuse to get away from the wives and drink a lot and bring in black whores, and then they would all go to church on Sunday. That was how South Africa was. It was, of course, impossible to film him whoring, but I thought that it was important to try to get that aspect of his personality. As you know, he subsequently went to prison and was only released a couple of days ago.[2] He was found guilty of the attempted murder of one of his servants, and his wife was always appearing wearing sunglasses to hide a black eye.

You were there for several weeks before you got to do the interview.
In a sense, it was taking the structure of *Waiting for Fidel* (1974) and applying it to Eugene Terre'Blanche, although in *Waiting for Fidel* the film-makers never actually met Castro. Michael Moore took the same structure in his film *Roger and Me* (1989). Every time Terre'Blanche snubbed us, it was great because it reinforced the fact that we were correct in the approach that we were taking. I was pleased and felt that the film was going really well in terms of getting a portrait of his followers and a portrait of Terre'Blanche's driver JP. JP was a much more complicated character than Terre'Blanche because he was funny and kind and compassionate and had a good relationship with his wife and kids. But he was lost and it was through JP that I really understood how fascism and its supporters came about in Nazi Germany. It

Terre'Blanche's 777 BMW,
The Leader, His Driver and the Driver's Wife

was people who had a lack of self-identity and a lack of a sense of self who went for an extreme ideology at a time when they needed some kind of certainty; I felt that this was a similar historical moment in South Africa, where people were clinging to anything they could. There was a fear on the left and on the right that they were going to be swept away on a torrent of blackness. A lot of people who hadn't received a great deal of education – someone like JP, who was trained as an electrician – became very right wing. This was not necessarily because they were anti-black; JP actually treated his servants really well and was a caring man. His wife also cared, but there was this odd situation in South Africa where you would have good relationships with black servants on a day-to-day level and yet if you asked JP about black government or black empowerment then he would come out with the most outrageous sentiments and say things that were deliberately shocking. At one point a journalist from *Time Out* came out to do a piece on us whilst we were making the film and JP immediately

started talking about making kaffir stew just to freak her out. I wanted this complexity to come out.

Eugene Terre'Blanche is a much more straightforward character. Emotionally he is a fascist and his day-to-day dealings with people were as a bully and as a fascist. You could see him taking enjoyment from beating people up and behaving like a Mussolini figure on his horse. I wanted to make something that would really puncture his balloon. In

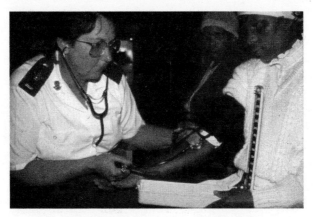

Anita, the driver's wife dispensing birth control,
The Leader, His Driver and the Driver's Wife

fact, I think that the greatest achievement of the film was the law case that arose at its completion over the film's assertion that Terre'Blanche was having a relationship with the journalist Jani Allan. There was a huge court case at the High Court and Channel Four spent over a million pounds just on getting the defence together, sending a lawyer and a researcher over to South Africa for five months to get information on Terre'Blanche. It emerged during the trial that they absolutely were having an affair, which was really the end of Terre'Blanche's support. The majority of his supporters were very high church, ultra-orthodox people who could not support a leader who was having an adulterous relationship.

How do you think Terre'Blanche will cope with the new South Africa he has recently been released into?
Most of the support for the AWB really came from the South African defence force, who would get them guns and explosives in their desperation at the last few years of the De Klerk regime to create outrages around the country. JP alludes to the fact that the tear gas he has comes from the defence force. I think that the bombs that were planted by Piet Rudolph also came from the defence forces, and there was really no attempt to bring these people to justice. Once the government changed and it was a black ANC government, the whole power base for the AWB disintegrated. They are now such a small and pathetic minority that I really can't see that they have any relevance at all.

The film catalogues this impending sense of demoralization and disillusionment. There is, for example, JP's feeling of betrayal when Piet Rudolph calls off his hunger strike.
JP was also quite a romantic man and really believed in the Boer 'Volk', that anything should be done for the 'Volk', including killing powerful political figures and sacrificing himself and his family if need be. JP actually sent me a death threat after the film. He warned me not to come back to South Africa because he would kill me. When I received the death threat, initially I was frightened but then I thought that they were such a hopeless bunch of people that they would be unable to organize a piss-up in a brewery. I mean, look at Terre'Blanche's army: there are supposed to be 10,000, but it is instead a pathetic handful of people. And the whole thing is shambolic, a bit like a Dad's Army that is taking itself much too seriously and has chosen a right-wing ideology.

The writing was really on the wall when there was an outrage in one of the townships just before the elections. AWB people had gone around threatening blacks and shooting at kids in buses, generally behaving in a very cowardly way towards people who were unarmed and not used to taking power into their own hands because for so long they had been downtrodden. But this carload of AWB members were in a township throwing their weight around when a group of blacks pulled out guns and mowed them down, killing them all. This act really had an incredible effect on the AWB because they were all cowards, so this was the last instance of them going into the townships in their khaki uniforms. They suddenly realized that this spell of being white and somehow untouchable was over. After that it was a whole different ball game.

It's a film of interesting juxtapositions with powerful use of voice-over. Accompanying panoramic travelling shots of the South African countryside and local music is a soundtrack in which you catalogue numerous recent white-on-black atrocities.
South Africa is a country of contradictions. It is one of the most beautiful countries I have been to and that red soil seeps into your bones and your psyche until you ache to have more of it. I would love to go back there. The size and beauty of it is intoxicating but at the same time it was populated by some of the most mean, narrow-minded and greedy people you could imagine. I suppose that having been so outnumbered, they devised this despicable ideology that supported their terrible behaviour.

I think that it was about this time that you began to use more music in your films.
I remember driving into a service station and there were these three black kids hunched over a ghetto blaster listening to township jive and I bought the tape off them. It was this tape that actually ended up in the film. I felt that the music had the spirit of Africa in it, as well as being really energetic. It made for amazing driving music and all the black kids were really into it. I also thought that the music, which drew upon numerous influences, was as representative of the new South Africa as the AWB was apt to listen to all those old Nazi marching songs.

How intense were the levels of intimidation? JP becomes sympathetic towards you after Barry Ackroyd is violently struck down by one of Terre'Blanche's cronies.

At some of the initial events we filmed, there was a strong feeling that some of these people felt besieged, alienated and frightened and that we may be somehow using their images to reveal who Terre'Blanche's supporters were. There was a terrible paranoia and that was why Barry was struck. And then, when we became friends with JP and started to hang out with him, we got to know all the main security guys in the AWB and also a lot of the more influential supporters. Many of these supporters preferred JP to Eugene and would much rather hang out at JP's house. As we were also hanging out at JP's, we gradually became friends with some of them. When we were at the large stadium at the end and Terre'Blanche was furious with us, there was a particularly violent confrontation where he said, 'Your camera-man is like a monkey hanging on a tree. He just won't put that thing down, just like a bloody monkey.' A number of his people wanted to beat me up but some of the security guards we knew told them to cool it and leave us alone. It could have turned very ugly as we were vastly outnumbered and a lot of these guys were spoiling for a fight with us as they perceived us to be reporting from a left-wing position. Barry did an amazing job, filming everything under very threatening circumstances.

All the men took a huge liking to Riete. Did this work in your favour?
We were certainly a curiosity in Ventersdorp, and it's a very cut-off little community. Half the women, in a rather repressed way, wanted to have an affair and there were a number of very wealthy guys who had made their fortune from the diamond mines and were looking for wives and who obviously thought that Riete was quite dishy. Riete, too, is a terrible flirt, educated and funny, so why shouldn't they be attracted to her?

You do a pretty good job of highlighting the ridiculousness of Terre'Blanche and his cronies, not just through the ill-attended rallies, but also in the surreal Bruce Springsteen covers-band sequence.
That was so weird. It was an AWB convention – which again was supposed to be so much bigger – and it felt like watching the last throes of a group of people who were in disarray. Springsteen was actually real-

ly supportive of the film because we had zero money to clear the rights of the track, but after explaining to him what the film was about and sending him a copy he gave us permission to use it. He appreciated the irony.

The outgoing South African government was incredibly corrupt, and in a sense *The Leader, His Driver* only touches the tip of it. For years the government had been funding these covert activities, including working out what the voodoo fears were in a particular area and then creating those fears to force people literally to run from their villages. De Klerk wanted to destabilize the country and it was only when he realized that he couldn't do it and it was inevitable that they were going to be replaced that he became very pragmatic and tried to create a takeover that was as smooth as possible. Up to that point, they fought it every step of the way.

In his speeches Terre'Blanche is fiercely critical of De Klerk.
A lot of white extremists thought that De Klerk had sold them out. Little did they realize that he had tried through various dirty-trick campaigns and other ways to play it as dirty as he could for as long as he could and then, when he recognized that there was no way he was going to win, he threw his hat in with the other crowd. This is, I suppose, what any politician would do.

You can't go into a country like South Africa without a pretty clear understanding of its political complexities. How long did you spend researching the project?
We did a lot of research, but I think that the film was basically just a lot of luck; we were in the right place at the right time. It was a historical moment and it was just providence that we were there to capture it just at the cusp. It was the right time to do it and I think that we took it on in the right spirit and with the right humour. It didn't become overly earnest by seeking to explain too much but treated the AWB in a manner that makes it difficult for you to take them too seriously.

Let's talk about the one-on-one interview with Terre'Blanche and your decision to arrive late.
I was very concerned not to give Terre'Blanche a political platform, so I wasn't that interested in really understanding his political position or

giving it a credibility that I didn't think it deserved. On the other hand, I wanted to get something that would reveal his temper and his bullying and the fact that he was just a thug. I felt that if I simply went to his office and did an interview with him, then he would simply repeat all the stuff that we had heard before – stuff like this was the land of his forefathers, that he would never accept Mandela and that he wanted a separate state. He was a good speaker and a powerful orator, so he could deliver all this in a manner that would somehow make it seem reasonable. And so I set an elephant trap.

Elephant traps are such fun because they are all to do with your knowledge of people, which becomes so intimate that you know exactly how they are going to react when you do something; so you find the simplest thing to trigger that reaction. In Eugene Terre'Blanche's case it was having a cup of tea in a café just up the road from his office, which we could actually see from the window, and waiting until we were ten to fifteen minutes late for the interview. He was such a self-important man with no sense of humour, and I remember Riete and Barry absolutely begging me to go because they knew how annoyed he would be. But I kept looking at my watch and saying, 'Let's just give it a couple of more minutes,' and by the time we got there Terre'Blanche had already left, indignant at the fact that we were late and despite the fact that this was an interview that we had been trying to arrange for weeks and that he had been cancelling all the time. But now that we were late and playing him at his own game he was furious. How could we be late, this incompetent bunch of Englanders?! He really hated the English more than anything, as did the majority of the white South Africans, a hatred that went right back to the Boer war. The English in South Africa lived down in the Cape, the more liberal part of the country, but here we were in the bastion of the Afrikaners, and he hated it. I'd also managed to insult their notions of masculinity by not consuming vast quantities of meat and beer in their presence, so they came to regard me as this pansy Englishman; telling Terre'Blanche that I was late because I was having a cup of tea really nailed it.

Although you did get the reaction you wanted, were you frightened at all?
I was shitting myself. I looked at the width of his arms – and his forearms, which were at least twice as thick as mine – and I started to

imagine what would happen if he leaned across the desk and punched me. I also looked for any doors out of his office because I was convinced that I would be able to run faster than him.

Then he misunderstands your first question and you refuse to let him get away with giving the answer that best suits his political motives.
That was the only question I was really interested in: at what point did Eugene Terre'Blanche feel that it was war and that it was impossible to work with the ANC? And how and when was he going to declare this war. He was so annoyed by this point that he couldn't hear the question and just wanted to put me down. 'Oh, you're not one of my generals, why should I tell you?' He didn't understand that I was asking a conceptual question. In a way, it was wonderful because it was a perfectly reasonable question, but he was unable to understand it.

You infuriate him still further by overtaking his car to get a passing shot on the way to a rally.
That was again just his massive ego. He didn't want to be overtaken in his very trendy little buggy. His ego was rattled when we zoomed past in our big old smoky VW combi. He would accelerate whenever we were trying to pass him. The wonderful thing about South Africa is that there is very little traffic so, as he accelerated, we would also accelerate until both cars were absolutely flat out with each of us inching forward. We'd be on the wrong side of the road and, in essence, playing chicken, but he just wouldn't back down.

So how did you get him on that occasion?
I sneaked up in his slipstream and then just floored it. Our van was also much heavier and I think we were going slightly downhill. We even waved as we went past.

Apart from the court case and the death threat from JP, what were the other repercussions from the film?
It had a very big effect on Eugene Terre'Blanche's standing and the extent to which he was taken seriously, particularly in South Africa, where he lost a lot of support. In fact, he lost his most credible support – that of the families – and was left only with a fractional fanatical element. He also lost his rank-and-file support; when he came out of prison there was an expectation that he would be met by a large num-

ber of supporters but there were only a handful, mainly because he had disappeared under such a cloud of disapproval from his own people.

The Leader, His Driver is a film that I am very fond of. Creatively, it worked out very well and I enjoyed adding the music. I think that a lot of the elements came together during the editing. I'm very hands-on during the editing and do pretty much most of the cuts myself. I had an incredible disagreement with John Mister, the film's editor. John is especially good at editing with music and really contributed to the film in terms of the music and the way it was used. But we really came to blows about the end of the film. I thought that it should end when it does, with the news that JP has left the party and that Eugene Terre'Blanche has driven into a river. It was a somewhat absurd ending and John wanted a much more melancholic ending to do with the history of the country. We had a big disagreement about it and I remember John showing the commissioning editor the two different endings when I wasn't around and trying to convince him that the ending I wanted was the wrong one. The film was initially mixed with John's alternate ending on it, and I wasn't happy with the result. I remember walking through Soho with Riete, with all the mixing elements in a huge plastic case, and we were literally knocking on the door of one mixing house after another and asking them if they had time to do the last five minutes of the film because we were on deadline in terms of having to deliver it. Finally, we found someone to do it. If I remember correctly, the person who did it was slightly under the influence.

Did you patch things up with John Mister?
Actually, no, because I felt that what he did was something that you just don't do. It's important that arguments remain within the cutting room. That was the last time that I worked with John, which is a pity because he is a wonderfully gifted editor and was also a close personal friend of mine. He had also made a great contribution to the editing of *Driving Me Crazy*. I guess I just felt very let down. This was also the last film that I cut in England for a very long time, obviously another reason why I didn't work again with John.

I carried on working with Riete for a while, but it was difficult given that she was also based in England, and as Barney was growing up and going to secondary school I felt that it was important that I remain in

America so that I could see him every day. Barney gave my life and my films a lot more purpose, so I took the decision to pretty much move my base to California entirely after *The Leader, His Driver*.

Your next film was a real departure for you. A filmed version of Spalding Gray's monologue about writer's block, Monster in a Box *was put together by producer Jon Blair, and you were brought in as a director-for-hire.*
It was very much Jon's project and he wanted to do it in a particular way: to shoot on 35mm, cut on tape and then blow up to 35mm. He reckoned he could save a lot of time doing it this way. Jon worked out the deal with Spalding and where and when the filming took place; he was a real producer.

I recall you saying that you had recently watched Monster in a Box *again and felt that you'd done a good job on it.*
I think I did. Jonathan Demme's *Swimming to Cambodia* (1987) was a more coherent piece and Demme certainly set the standard for how the film was going to be done. It was my blueprint and we used Laurie Anderson, who did the music on *Swimming To Cambodia*, as we did Skip Lievsay, who did the sound. It was very much the intention to take the model of Demme's film and transplant it to *Monster in a Box*.

Why did Jon Blair choose you for the assignment?
According to Jon, it was because Spalding Gray and his wife Renée Shafransky liked my work and were very interested in working with me. In a way, I was a curious choice. Jon is an interesting man, complicated and quite hard to read, but in a way I think that our collaboration worked out. He has done some very prestigious films, but is actually very self-effacing and very fascinated with the technical aspects of film-making. This surprised me because I'm just not. Anyway, I'm surprised by how well we pulled the film off. It's a well-thought-through piece and very relaxed; it shows what a great artist Spalding is.

It was made very cheaply, which partly explains why the edit was so stressful, and shot over three performances, with just half a day for pick-ups and any special effects. It was a very good exercise because I had to be very prepared, which is not something I always am. I really studied the show and had filmed earlier shows. It was quite hard to instruct the camera team – we had mics and headphones – and I

Monster in a Box

remember on the day that we shot I introduced Spalding to the audience at the Riverside Studios in Hammersmith and then, as Spalding sat down to start the show, I rushed up to get into the box to give instructions to the camera people, only to find that the door to the box was locked. I couldn't go back because that would have necessitated my walking onto the stage, so I was banging on the door, and meanwhile the show had started. It was half an hour before I got in and everyone was just merrily filming away. I realized at that moment how totally irrelevant directors are, but it all worked out well.

I did find editing from tape a little frustrating because you couldn't accurately tell how sharp some of the images were; so you are working off a degraded image, as opposed to working from film, and this is one of the reservations I have concerning that whole digital revolution. DV is still not in any way as sharp and defined or layered as film and so it's rather odd that one's regressed on such a major level. I really felt as though I was working with a sub-standard image. However, it's a process I have repeated, cutting *Biggie and Tupac* and *Aileen: The Selling of a Serial Killer* on Avid, but I don't like the process of editing that way. I know a lot of directors prefer to cut on film – Fred Wiseman, for example. I have lots of Steenbecks and still feel that I can get a better film when I edit on one of those. I also prefer the more physical aspect of editing on film, winding and moving the cans around. Working on something like the Avid is basically just typing with your fingers. I like to move around a lot when I edit and always choose big editing rooms with a window and a view. I always think that editing should be the best aspect of the film. When we edited *Soldier Girls*, Joan and I would start early in the morning and have a game of tennis at lunchtime, which would invariably relax us, calm us down and put us in a good mood. Editing is also that time when you get to know the material even better, teasing out and finding its hidden secrets and the inner logic that may perhaps have previously eluded you. It's important to be receptive. You really have to revisit a scene five or six times to fully understand what information you are using that scene to convey, and the information you wish it to convey may alter during the process of editing it. Cutting from film enables you to do this as the process necessitates watching the scene that you are editing over and over again, as opposed to the Avid, which revolves much more around making much shorter selects.

Did the experience of making Lily Tomlin *make you reluctant to accept the* Monster in a Box *assignment?*
I did fear that it would be a boring performance piece and could be quite dull. I was again working with cinematographer Mick Coulter, whom I'd had a disastrous experience with on *Diamond Skulls*. We had, however, remained good friends, though it was undoubtedly the worst film in both our careers. *Monster in a Box* is beautifully shot and beautifully lit, and I think that the setting brought out the best in both of us as Mick likes a very controlled environment for his lighting and likes to have his cameras on dollies.

Were you an admirer of Spalding Gray's work before making the film?
I was. I'd seen *Swimming to Cambodia* but I also felt that we were similar in that we both, in a sense, made diaries of our lives with our work – especially after *Driving Me Crazy* – in order to consider how it moved our lives forward. Spalding's monologues were very much about that and in *Monster in a Box* he talks about why he was having such problems writing this book. It's related to his wrestling with the problem of his mother's suicide and the way in which his everyday life and his relationship with his wife Renée all impinge on his ability to write. That adds the humour, the frustration and compassion to the piece. I feel that I have done a similar thing with films, in that I have gone into the problems that I have had whilst making them and used that as a way of defining the subject. There was certainly a symmetry to the way we work.

I think you both also look at the veneer of fame and celebrity.
I guess so. This is connected to the kind of person Spalding was. With Lily Tomlin, I could never actually discuss her show because she would hyperventilate if she thought I was criticizing it, whereas with Spalding and Renée you could have real discussions. I remember thinking that Spalding's show was half an hour too long, and so we talked about cutting it and I was able to argue my points through with Spalding and Renée. We worked things through very logically and very quickly. They were both completely open to suggestions and were concerned about working to create a better piece.

What suggestions did you make in terms of visualizing the monologue?

I was very certain about wanting to do something with the moments in the monologue where Spalding has to switch between a conversation between two different people. For these moments I wanted him to do the different speeches to two different cameras, flicking backwards and forwards between the two. He's so good at doing that. He's a brilliant monologist and also a very accomplished actor. It was a real pleasure working with Spalding, despite the fact that his relationship with Renée was coming apart a little at that point and there was a certain amount of tension. Fortunately, the majority of the film was done before things got really tense or it would certainly have been harder to work with them. Renée was very much Spalding's anchor and mainstay, grounding him and creating a good environment for him to work in. She protected him, and though I think that Spalding felt that he was overprotected in terms of his work, it was fantastic.

I don't know why, but I'm surprised that the show was filmed in the UK. I guess it does say something about the universal appeal of Spalding's work.
I think that Spalding's monologue is very much the dilemma of any writer in terms of trying to deal with their own demons and family histories.

In the monologue Spalding talks very humorously about wanting to spend a Christmas working with potential suicides. Given recent events, this takes on a very poignant resonance.[3]
That's what really affected me when I watched the film again the other day. Spalding's own suicide is implicit in the monologue. It's his obsession. His mother committing suicide had such a profound effect on him and was deep in his psyche. It was an option that Spalding continually wrestled with.

It's amazing how much it also crossed over into his other acting work. One of his best acting jobs was in Steven Soderbergh's King of the Hill *(1993), in which he plays a man who ends up committing suicide.*
I met Spalding at the Tribeca festival not that long ago, but just afterwards Spalding was involved in a car accident in Ireland and received a very bad head injury, as well as damaging one side of his body, so restricting his mobility. He was very upset at this Tribeca event because he couldn't dance, which was something he absolutely loved

to do. At any party he would always end up with the most attractive woman and would then dance all night in the most wild and cavalier fashion, like a rather mad Cossack. He was so involved in his own pain that he couldn't see the pain he was causing his wife, the mother of his two children. Spalding had always been able to internalize his pain and anguish into his monologues but the head injury affected his memory so he wasn't able to do that on this occasion. The monologues were very much his therapy, turning his demons and his agonies into artistic triumphs. I wasn't that surprised to hear of his suicide.

So Monster in a Box *is a film that you were happy with, both artistically and in terms of the experience of making it. Was this view echoed by Spalding and Renée?*
I think so, though *Swimming to Cambodia* was the most successful and was less bitty than *Monster in a Box*, which was broken up because it was also a play within a play that takes us to various different continents and locations in quite an episodic way. I remember finding the material quite thematically dispersed, even though it all happened in the time that he was trying to write this book; though the individual episodes are all great, I felt that Demme's film was more coherent. I've not seen Soderbergh's *Gray's Anatomy* (1996) so I can't comment on how that compares.

Would you revisit doing something in a similar format?
I think I would. I enjoyed it and think that I have the confidence to do it now. These things are fun to do now and again because they don't take as long as the more personal works and don't require the same degree of self-sacrifice. You don't feel that you are having to constantly put yourself on the line, hoping that it will work out. The other films are not as much fun to do, but they are perhaps more enriching in other ways.

Something of a flipside to The Leader, His Driver and the Driver's Wife, Too White for Me *takes a close look at Chicco Twala, a renowned black South African musician born in Soweto. An affectionate portrait of a man full of contradictions – Chicco is closely aligned with both Nelson and Winnie Mandela but lives by his own gangster code – Broomfield's film also reveals a deeply troubled nation at a time of massive social, political and racial change.*

Chicco Twala, *Too White For Me*

Was Too White for Me *a project that naturally evolved out of making* The Leader, His Driver?

Yes, it did, and mainly out of my buying that cassette from those kids. I thought that it would be fantastic to get into their world, and just as *Behind the Rent Strike* was the answer to *Proud to Be British*, *Too White for Me* was going to be the answer to *The Leader, His Driver*. I also wanted to try and release a record that would come out with the film so that there would be a soundtrack featuring the local band Splash, but the trouble was that the band weren't a very interesting group of guys. They were very close to the white record company and were very successful in a white puritanical way, driving BMWs, etc., but there was something Uncle Tom-like about them and the white record executives would snigger at them. I didn't feel that much empathy for the guys. However, there was this other guy, Chicco Twala, who was slightly older than Splash but also a real gangster. His brother had been killed by gangsters in Soweto. He was very involved up with the ANC, he had put up guerrillas, he was a close personal friend of Nelson Mandela and, like many others, had had an affair with Winnie when Mandela was in prison. He was just a wonderful guy and a real rogue. He was always up to skulduggery or high jinks of one sort or another and we got on immediately. Chicco's music was an extension of all that. His record company hated him as they just thought of him as a gangster; well, he did carry a pistol under his shirt and had an AK47 in his car, but I loved him.

The problem with the film, really, was that the music side was very weak when it should have been very strong. This was because we could never really mic the concerts properly, and what I really should have done was get a sound engineer from the UK because the equipment there wasn't good enough. The concerts were organized by a brewery company and were always incredibly chaotic as everyone was drunk before the concerts even started. Chicco never knew before his band went on stage how many people would be playing, so it was impossible to mic everybody, and then they would all be on this tiny stage stoned and drunk out of their minds. It was utter chaos. The experience of making the film was really interesting, but I don't feel that it's a great film. It's an interesting character study but I would have liked it to be much deeper. The politics didn't really come through either; I should have pushed that aspect harder. In hindsight, I should have been clearer about the film's political agenda and made more of my connections with Nelson and Winnie Mandela, both of whom I met. It was such a great opportunity and I think it's safe to say I blew it because I was so wedded to the idea of making a music film.

I had always wanted to make a music film and spent a lot of time with The Clash before all these films. I even started going on tour with them when I was going to do a film for a TV company circa 1980. I loved their performances – though they did blow my hearing – and I think that this was a film that I could have done really well. It was all going to be done through Bernie Rhodes, but then Bernie got the sack and former journalist Caroline Coon took over. I didn't really take to

Caroline, and she didn't get what I was trying to do with the film. Bernie really got what I wanted to do.

What did you want to do exactly? Because a Clash film did come out shortly after.
That's right, *Rude Boy* (1980) by Jack Hazan and David Mingay. They objected to my film happening as they feared it would interfere with theirs; in fact, I think they threatened to chuck their film in the bin. That's a pretty treacherous thing to do and I would never do that to another film-maker. My attitude has always been let the best man win. We are in the business of the survival of the fittest and their film was going to be so very different to mine. Perhaps they could even have complemented each other. My film would have been influenced by Robert Frank's *Cocksucker Blues* (1972), which was a real look at the Stones on tour. I wanted to do something much more like that. Their performances were brilliant and I think we could have done a really great film. I would also have included material concerning the band's relationship with Bernie Rhodes, a really exuberant and completely honest guy who I liked very much. I really regret that the film never happened. Julien Temple also did some filming with The Clash. Julien was at the film school after me, but I remember seeing some of his film and thinking that it was really good. Then, of course, Julien did The Sex Pistols and lost interest in The Clash, quite wrongly. I think he felt that The Clash were inferior to The Sex Pistols, but history has shown that this just isn't true.

So I had really wanted to do a music film and thought that *Too White for Me* was going to be this opportunity. But again it eluded me and the film didn't really work. *Kurt and Courtney* also started off as being much more of a film about the music that had inspired Kurt Cobain and the musicians that were still playing in Seattle. I was then prevented from making that film too and forced into something very different and making a much more aggressive film than I intended. *Too White for Me*? A bit of a mess, to be honest.

I think that some of the political stuff and the racial tensions come across well. At one point Chicco exclaims, 'What have the whites ever done for us? Fuck the whites.'
Chicco is the new black middle class. I haven't looked at the film for a while, but my memory of it is that it is unclear conceptually, certainly

not as clear as *The Leader, His Driver*, and is just not one of my better films.

A lot of people had warned you off working with Chicco, claiming that he was dangerous and not to be trusted. I think that the worst aspect of his character is his antiquated views on women.
Well, he's a very traditional man. Like a lot of those guys, Chicco had made his money but was educationally quite traditional. In a sense, he desired the best of both worlds; he wanted to have as many women as he could, but at the same time he was quite sophisticated and was a very astute businessman. Undoubtedly he had a pretty crazy temper and would frequently get really angry with some of his servants and with Tembe, his wife, but that is probably not surprising when you have grown up in Soweto in such a violent environment. He was also left very upset by the killing of his brother; essentially he was a good guy who was trying to do his best for his family. I can only imagine what it must have been like to grow up at the time of turmoil when the white government was at its most extreme in terms of trying to hang onto its power. That atmosphere is bound to produce a very convoluted person and, in a way, I was surprised by how open and refreshing Chicco was, but the film didn't translate itself as easily as *The Leader, His Driver*, which was a much simpler scenario and documented a very clear political position. Chicco's position was more complicated as he was neither one thing nor the other. He wasn't really a new South African because he had so many legacies from the old regime. He was certainly responsible for killing the people responsible for his brother's death and, I think, half tortured them.

If I'd formalized things more through Chicco, it would have been a very original way to Nelson and Winnie, and then it would have been a pretty amazing film. Someone of good authority told me that Chicco in actual fact may have been one of the main drug dealers for the ANC before they came to power, and it was with this money that the ANC bought guns and explosives to fight their cause.

Did you encounter antagonism from some of Chicco's people? You say in the film that they perhaps equated you with the Boers because you were white.
Undoubtedly. One of the things they most enjoyed doing was watching *The Leader, His Driver* whilst getting stoned and drinking beer and screaming with laughter. There was no getting around the fact

that I was white and they were black. We used to go to clubs with Chicco, clubs that we would never ordinarily get into, and the situations that arose were sometimes quite fun, such as black girls coming on to you, but also quite scary.

Was there not also a pretty hairy episode when you picked up a couple of dangerous hitch-hikers?
Chicco was very freaked out in Soweto because he had killed a lot of people there and feared the vengeance of the families and friends of his victims. There he would be very armed and very paranoid. As we were driving along in Soweto I spotted a couple hitch-hiking and so I stopped. Chicco, who was in the car in front of us, screeched to a halt and turned round and sped back to us. He jumped out of the car with his revolver out, shouting and screaming. I thought that he had really gone too far this time. I mean, I was just giving someone a lift but Chicco ran up to one of the guys who was about to get into the car and stuck his pistol to the back of the guy's head. The guy opened up his long coat to reveal a sawn-off shotgun. Afterwards, Chicco really shouted at me, explaining that the guy was a car-jacker and would have stolen my car and then undoubtedly killed me.

A close shave.
It was, although I've always been quite charmed in that way, often feeling as if there is a protective angel looking after me. To a certain extent you have to believe that, doing what I do. You also have to try to believe in the more positive aspects of human nature to convince you that everything is going to be all right. It would be easy to get into these situations and get killed. There was the film recently, for example, *Death in Gaza* (2004), in which the director died.4

Did Chicco see the finished film?
He did, though as part of my deal with him it was never officially screened in South Africa. I never spoke to Chicco directly about it, but heard that he had found it funny but also slightly painful. We have continued to be in touch and I regard Chicco and Tembe as friends. Chicco is such a scallywag, I would love to see him.

Were the concerts that took place stacked more in favour of the white performers and the white audiences?

Completely. The selections and the billing were loaded to the white audiences, and on the part of the promoters there was very little interest in getting the township people along. The headliners would invariably be these not especially talented white musicians, with Chicco and other really acclaimed black talents the sideshow. There was a real racism going on here, not least because the black musicians were also being paid so much less money.

You thank Joan Churchill in the closing credits.
I'm not entirely sure why, to be honest. I don't think that she was involved in the shoot.

Notes

1. www.nickbroomfield.com.
2. Jailed in March 2001 for beating one of his farm workers so badly that the man was brain-damaged, Terre'Blanche also served six months in 2000 for assaulting a petrol-station attendant and setting his dog on him. The leader of the AWB (Afrikaner Resistance Movement) was freed from jail on Friday 11 June 2004. Upon release he was met by a small group of supporters as he rode through the streets of Potchefstroom, a conservative town about sixty miles west of Johannesburg. Allegedly, resounding jeers greeted the parade.
3. The body of Spalding Gray was recovered from the East River in New York on 9 March 2004. Gray was sixty-two years old.
4. A harrowing documentary that portrays the horror of the conflict in Israeli/Palestine. Director James Miller was killed during the making of the film.

5

Sex and Power

*Tracking Down Maggie, Heidi Fleiss:
Hollywood Madam, Fetishes*

Mark and Margaret,
Tracking Down Maggie

Building upon the structure so effectively explored in The Leader, His Driver and The Driver's Wife, Tracking Down Maggie *shows Nick Broomfield in dogged pursuit of an interview with former British prime minister Margaret Thatcher as she undertakes numerous American engagements to promote her book* The Downing Street Years. *Building up a detailed account of Thatcher's family background and personality – courtesy of numerous former, frequently eccentric neighbours and reluctant family members – Broomfield also uncovers a number of damning facts relating to Thatcher's involvement in various lucrative arms deals, invariably involving her multi-millionaire son, Mark.*

JW: *You certainly put yourself on the line in* Tracking Down Maggie. *You begin the film by stating that you have always been interested in Thatcher, but I don't imagine that you were an admirer.*

NB: I was not an admirer. With Thatcher, it was the feeling that this woman had somehow dominated our lives through a very bleak time and created a major reversal of attitude, the legacy of which we are still dealing with. I'm sure that Thatcher is a much greater inspiration to Tony Blair than any of the great Labour leaders. It was very much trying to understand for myself what her ideology really was, to try and get a sense of who this woman was, where she had come from, what it was that made her think the way she thought and to also capture something of her personal relationships, be it with her cabinet or with her son and her daughter. I wanted to understand what kind of human being she was to advocate, in so articulate a way, such a greedy, selfish and rather inhuman philosophy.

Although it's not actually in the film – and I regret that it isn't – there is a scene with Archbishop Runcie, who had been at Oxford with Thatcher and had taught her bible classes in which he remembers their sitting down and studying the New and Old Testaments. Whereas she had a complete understanding of the Old Testament – with its emphasis on retribution and vengeance and so on – when it came to the New Testament and its more sophisticated and forgiving Christian values, including learning from the suffering of others and expressing compassion and pity, he drew an absolute blank. Because the Labour party were in such disarray and were unable to form any kind of unified voice, it was actually the Church of England who almost provided the best voice of opposition, on strictly Christian values, against the inhumanity of Margaret Thatcher's policies. I am talking about her dealing with the homeless, those people who couldn't gain employment and those suffering from mental illness. She had absolutely no interest in the casualties of our society. When Thatcher came into power, she redefined those old paternalistic Tory values that had lasted from the Second World War. When the war finished, there was a belief that we should build homes for heroes and that we should create a society that reflected that. Even Macmillan and the rest were paternalistic Tories who took their responsibilities very seriously and, compared to the Americans, were raving pinkos. And then Thatcher came along and changed all that, labelling them 'wets' and insulting their masculinity. She was a terrifying woman.

Did the film become a very different one as it unfolded? I mean, Thatcher would have dug less of a grave for herself if she'd just agreed to an interview with you and talked. The longer she evades you, the more murky information about her nepotistic arms dealings you manage to dredge up.

Thatcher was used to total control. She had very little humour about herself and wanted to control every word that was written about her. That's evident from all the interviewers that she knighted – Sir Robin Day, for example. They were at Thatcher's beck and call and were the only ones that ever got interviews. They were pretty respectful on the whole. They didn't really dare give her what I term a ropey-dopey, to get her on the ropes and batter her to death.

Do you think that Thatcher underestimated you?

I think that she was just used to things she ignored going away, and what I really hope is that when all the sickly epitaphs that we will no doubt read when she dies have gone away, my film will be part of her legacy and that people will remember her in the way the film portrays her. People also need to recover from the Thatcherite legacy that privatization is a good thing; I really don't think it is. A lot of the abuses that we saw happening in places like Iraq are perpetuated through private firms and a lot of the abuses that we saw happening in Bosnia were through the private security firms that are not controllable in the same way that you would want in a democracy. Thatcher represents the extreme of the pendulum in that for years we had rather extreme and petty trade unions in power; her reaction to that was to neuter the Labour movement – and to forget all the fantastic legislation and the humanity that had been brought in to protect people against those out for a quick buck – and to forcibly introduce all this privatization that we are suffering from at the moment in this incredibly greedy world. Hopefully, we're at the end of the cycle of the abuses Thatcher and Ronald Reagan brought in and we are about to start going back in the other direction.

As part of Thatcher's legacy we must remember the incredible government corruption; by that I am specifically referring to arms deals like Al Yamamah,[1] which was negotiated by Thatcher and which her son Mark managed to cash in on. This was the result of incredible nepotism. We should also remember the corruption whereby Thatcher was enabling various American arms to come into Britain and then enjoy transit to various parts of the world – including the selling of chemical weapons to Iraq – because parliamentary vetting of these deals was so much laxer than Congress. There was a contempt for democracy. Thatcher was far from a natural democrat and was very much of the 'I know best and I'll tell you what to do' school; I think that when people turned on her at the end she was genuinely amazed and dumbfounded and felt that people were very ungrateful. There was a marked lack of belief in democratic principles, and not only in the way that she ran her cabinet, which was rather like a boarding-school matron telling her pupils how to do things. She surrounded herself with yes-men who finally found the balls to get rid of her. I think you can see that even though Tony Blair is ostensibly Labour, it is the same form of government; there is the same lack of belief in democracy, and I think there have been abuses all around the world because of that. Far from Thatcher being a figure who should be emulated, she should be put in the dungeon of horrors.

Another criticism frequently levelled at you is that your films reveal more about you than they do about the subject the film is purporting to cover. But Tracking Down Maggie *is a film that very carefully and very eloquently lays out the facts about Thatcher's moral, financial and political improprieties and how these lead to Britain becoming the second biggest arms exporter in the world following the Falklands War. Does the oft-repeated criticism irk you, though?*[2]
I'm certainly aware of it but have never really understood it and would be really interested to know what they mean. With any film that they might choose to mention, I would argue very strongly that it's nothing more than a device. In this particular film, there's no other way of telling the story when you are confronted with somebody who absolutely refuses to be interviewed and who refuses to talk about these issues. The only way to do it is to use yourself as this character who is investigating Margaret Thatcher and coming up with all this stuff. There's just no other way of structuring it that I can think of.

You also go back to Thatcher's home town to reveal details about her childhood and her desire to hide her roots by taking elocution lessons. You present irrefutable facts about her that have nothing to do with you or your desire to interview Thatcher on camera.
True, but I also don't think the same can be said of *The Leader, His Driver* either. That film is very much about Eugene Terre'Blanche and not at all about me. Neither of the Aileen Wuornos films are about me, so I really just don't get it. I thought it was really amusing in that recent Anthony Andrews piece in the *Observer* on Michael Moore when Moore indicated to the writer that I took great pleasure in appearing in my films. Some gall, I thought, especially as Michael appears far more in his films than I do in mine.

Tracking Down Maggie *also reveals the extent to which the British media have continued to contribute to her wealth and pander to her power. You detail the BBC paying £300,000 to the Thatcher foundation to get access to her.*
It's scandalous, and because people were so frightened of her, because she was such a bully, there was an unquestioning acceptance of her

behaviour. She evoked the thirty-year rule so we will never know what really happened in many of the arms deals; there has been a closure of the files. As I said earlier, it has encouraged a form of corruption on a worldwide scale that we are still suffering from now.

Were you frightened and intimidated by Thatcher?
I wasn't intimidated by her because she has an arrogance that demands to be argued with. I'd only want to argue with her if I had a lot of facts at my fingertips and could have a bit of fun with it because she is very good at pushing a point. Once she has seen that she has a point she will just carry on pushing into you, and that's what she does to terrify people. I mean, look at the episode with Sir Robin Day. She looks like great fun to argue with because she is humourless, and if you can keep skipping around and jabbing at things she doesn't expect, then she's at a complete loss.

The Iron Lady: Baroness Thatcher,
Tracking Down Maggie

There's a by turns amusing and infuriating moment when your car is alongside her car and you tap on the window and call her name, only for her to pretend that you don't exist.

That's what she's very good at; that is what she has done for her entire political career. Anything she didn't like, she didn't hear.

You've talked about the process of coming across a moment that you know is pure gold and will be brilliant in a film. Such a moment in Tracking Down Maggie *is the woman you interview who has Thatcher's old loo.*

The woman was one of those wonderful English eccentrics. She had found Thatcher's loo in a skip outside her house and taken it home and put a plaque above it proclaiming that 'Margaret Thatcher sat here'. A lot of people have a reverence for Margaret Thatcher because they don't really understand her political philosophy, which basically came from the belief that if people have a great deal of wealth then there will be a trickle-down effect that will somehow imbue the rest of the population with money. This is absolutely false. People are greedy and it doesn't happen. If you look at the world today, the disparity between the rich and the poor has never been greater, and a lot of the problems around the world can be traced to the vast numbers of workers forced to endure slave-labour conditions and payment. This is a direct result of Thatcher's policies; it's a complete lack of responsibility from the so-called western democracy to the rest of the world. The motivation is profit and greed, and this comes directly from Margaret Thatcher and Ronald Reagan, and until there is a fundamental change in the philosophy of these two countries then these global problems are not going to go away.

Like Soldier Girls, Tracking Down Maggie *is very much a film of characters. We have Thatcher, Elizabeth the press officer, the detective who you nickname 'sniffer of the yard'. It's a film of great characters and you structure the film around them, but then it all becomes more sinister once you get hold of Thatcher's US schedule. Suddenly you fear that your phone is tapped, you are hounded from hotels and an air of paranoia ensues. You even introduce some quite moody music and replay material for the viewer to reveal important details they may have previously overlooked.*

It was a deliberate technique once it got under way, but it actually happened by accident. I was having terrible trouble editing the film. The original editor had a premature birth halfway through the edit, leaving me without an editor. Then there was an earthquake and shortly thereafter I had to go to Canada to give an award. When I tried to get back to America I was prevented from entering because I was only on a tourist visa. They discovered that I owned a house in California, so I had to go to the TV company I was working for and get them to get me a journalist's visa. It was while I was waiting and stuck in a hotel room in Toronto that I went over the structure of the film, as I had the transcripts of me. I kept asking myself, 'What is it that I'm interested in?' Sometimes the great thing about documentary is that, because you are dealing with real things and with your experience of making the film, when you are having a real problem in the editing room you can stop to ask yourself what thoughts were going through your head at the time. I always keep a little notebook that I write things down in during the films and I remembered feeling quite paranoid and I remembered 'sniffer' wandering around. Wherever you looked, you had a feeling that he would be there. He was like a hound dog and a right shifty little bugger.

With regard to the air of paranoia, when you start dealing with the arms business – which is directly related to the drugs business – you start interacting with characters who are off normal legal limits: people in the secret service, drug dealers, Mossad, the CIA and all those people who are in that quasi-legal and quasi-illegal world where human life doesn't mean anything at all. By and large, we live in a world where there is a pretence that human life means something, but in reality human life means absolutely nothing and is eminently expendable. There were a number of journalists who had been carrying out similar investigations who had been killed; in fact, one who was investigating the supply of weapons to Iraq was killed and later found in a hotel-room cupboard. Normal legal rules do not apply and you suddenly can't get information. You are aware that there are other people who know what is going on, but you are not getting the information out of them because there are other things at risk.

I think there are parallels with Thatcher and Eugene Terre'Blanche. There is something of the bully about them both. You also show them both to be apt to dig their own holes and appear to ever dwindling audiences.

Thatcher reminds me more of Ronald Reagan in that he seems to be such a revered figure and yet was such a corrupt man. Apart from a book titled *Dark Victory*,[3] there has been very little real overt criticism of him. There were some films made about him but these were taken off television as there is a kind of censorship, and that, in a way, applies to Margaret Thatcher. It's also harder to criticize Thatcher now because she is old and doddery and recently lost her husband, but I hope that at the point where she dies she will be re-evaluated and that the excesses and the corruptions that happened whilst she was in power will be brought to light.

I was reminded of Peter Moore's 'fly in the ointment' comment again when you refuse to turn off your cameras when Thatcher is giving a dinner speech and you are thrown out of that hotel in Dallas – but not before you ask if you can keep the complimentary straw Stetsons.
They were going crazy. They were so angry! This was one of those films when one had to have a lot of fun and I wonder now if some of the films didn't suffer from being more serious.

You also upset the applecart by deviating from protocol and asking Thatcher a question whilst she is visiting the Holocaust museum. She chides you like a child before just walking off. Did it take gall to ask a question at this moment?
It did a bit, and the other journalists were all pissed off because this was their opportunity to ask questions and she just walked off. The shortest press conference in history. I was also criticized because I did it at the Holocaust museum, but I think that it is precisely that kind of policy – namely, the indiscriminate sale of arms to peoples around the world – that causes holocausts and the bloodshed and the genocide that we saw in Iraq under Saddam Hussein. I thought that it was absolutely relevant to ask a question at the Holocaust museum.

It strikes me that in the case of Thatcher and with many other figures in your films you are constantly drawn to dominating people in positions of authority. Why do you feel this to be?
History tends to be determined by people in authority. People making rules, influencing decisions and creating trends. So, as a documentarian documenting contemporary history, I am naturally drawn to them.

At the close of the film you finally confront Julian Seymour, Thatcher's oily press aide, who has been systematically ignoring your phone messages. Was it satisfying to finally get him on camera?
It's an absurd moment, isn't it? I always wanted to really clobber Margaret Thatcher, so Julian Seymour was second best.

It's amazing the way he boldly lies on camera, maintaining that he has returned every one of your calls.
He was just a complete liar and utterly shameless.

Riete Oord and Barry Ackroyd are two people that you have enjoyed a long working relationship with.
I certainly couldn't have made the film without Riete because, through a contact of hers, she was able to get Margaret Thatcher's schedule. Riete is a great laugh to work with, and Riete and Barry are both close friends; they both made a fantastic contribution. They draw the trust and respect of people. They have a great ability to make friends with the subjects, a most important part of making a film. I think that Barry found these films hard work, because you do work incredibly long hours and never really know where you are going to be from one day to the next. This makes things quite stressful on a psychological level. We did have a good period of time together, making *The Leader, His Driver, Too White for Me, Tracking Down Maggie* and then *Aileen Wuornos: The Selling of a Serial Killer*. *Heidi Fleiss: Hollywood Madam* was the big change because it represents a new era in a way and another new style.

When was the last time you saw Tracking Down Maggie?
I saw some of it quite recently at a film festival in Norway of all places and I was surprised how kind of Michael Moore a lot of the gags are. It's full of gags and generally quite comedic, probably the most so of all those films. I mainly remember my frustrations with Thatcher, so I did find it very amusing to look at. I think it's a film that will stand the test of time and that does deal with a very painful part of her legacy.

Were there repercussions at the time for making it?
I remember that the Channel Four lawyers were very worried, particularly about some of the arms allegations. I think I had to make a few minor changes, but there was actually very little comment on it. A

member of my family who is in the army and deals with arms-related matters and who knew a lot of the people the film was referring to was really surprised that we got away with it.

You say that you recently saw part of the film in Norway. How is your international standing? You are obviously well-known in the UK and America, but how is your work viewed in a wider sense?
The films have sold pretty much in all the countries, and certainly throughout most of Europe and Australia. Latin America is quite a hard market to crack. I was invited to Argentina this year, but was unable to go. It is useful to go to these festivals, especially if you can get into the mainstream press as it is a way of getting your work out there a bit more. It's important that you choose films that mean something to people around the world.

A warts-and-all look at high-class prostitution, Broomfield's Heidi Fleiss: Hollywood Madam *is also a gripping and suitably sleazy exposé of LA mores and Hollywood types. Featuring an extensive interview with Heidi herself – at the time of filming facing jail for her part in running a top-end call-girl service – the film also features interviews with Heidi's former lover Ivan Nagy and her one-time business partner and confidante, Madam Alex. This was also the first of Broomfield's films to tenaciously explore the links between the LAPD and organized crime.*

Heidi Fleiss: Hollywood Madam *contains such a vast array of characters that I had to very carefully note them all down. There's obviously Heidi Fleiss, the fairly repulsive Ivan Nagy, the shadowy and rather fearsome Cookie, Heidi's former colleague Madam Alex, and ex-LAPD detectives Mike Brambles and Daryl Gates. Given the shadowy LA underworld you delve into, at times it felt like watching something scripted by Raymond Chandler.*
I was actually introduced to the project by my son Barney, who chose to write about Heidi Fleiss for a school project. It was a current story in all the newspapers at the time and I had helped him do some research. About six months later I was trying to think of ideas for films, partly because of my domestic situation: I was being a father, Barney was going to school in LA and I had relatively recently bought a house there, so I decided that I really wanted to do something that was based around Los Angeles. I'd always worked elsewhere and felt

Heidi Fleiss, *Heidi Fleiss: Hollywood Madam*

that I wanted to do an LA story and to learn about the city. These were my main reasons for doing it.

LA is very different from other cities. People have mainly gone there for a very specific reason, and that reason is to make it in the entertainment business, but only about 0.5 per cent make it. The rest are bus boys with scripts or they're cleaners who go to auditions, and some of the ones who are less successful are prostitutes. In Los Angeles everybody has their price and people are valued very much on the kind of car they drive and where they live; it is, without doubt, the most materialistic city I have ever lived in. Even though it is surrounded by the most fabulous landscape – you can see mountains when there isn't smog – very few people are really enjoying it. Although it has this myth of being quite a laid-back environment with everybody getting together around the pool and smoking joints, it is the most driven city I've ever been to. People go to bed early and drug-free because they are so motivated towards success, so I wanted to make a film that was a statement about that mentality and those people.

Heidi Fleiss symbolized that. She came from a fairly well-to-do family;

her father was a very well-known paediatrician who was well-respect-
ed within the community. He was actually a very unlikely LA character and was very much a socialist who gave a lot of his time to social
causes. And yet Heidi herself was very attracted to the money of LA,
to the wealth. She is really in love with money. It is Heidi's passion. LA
is also full of young beautiful women from all around America; it is
something like a Third Reich dream of a gene pool made up of all the
beautiful people in America. Because these women have gone there to
make it but very few of them do, what happens is that all the dweeby
guys – who could never pull a great girl at high school but have now
made it one way or another in the film business – can suddenly acquire
all these wonderful young girls. Heidi would act as a facilitator
between these older, generally rather geeky guys and these absolutely
ravishingly gorgeous girls who would never normally be with these
guys were it not for the fact that they are in LA and their ambition has
overtaken every other desire. That's the basis of the film. All the
Raymond Chandler characters literally crawled out of the woodwork.
I had no idea about characters such as Cookie. Cookie turned out to
be allegedly the biggest ecstasy dealer in the US.

*Everyone is absolutely terrified of Cookie. One young woman refuses
to speak on camera about what he did to her.*
He certainly beats people up and kills people. He also threatens to put
some pellets up my ass when I talk to him. The film was really difficult
to do one way or another, but I'm actually really proud of it because I
felt that it had a *Rashomon*-type structure with me going round talking to all these liars and everybody spinning a different story. Heidi,
Ivan and Madam Alex – they were all incredible talkers. All the people within this world basically just call each other up on the phone and
tell lies, half-truths intermingled with their intermittently threatening
each other and, in a way, the structure of the film really buys into all
that. I was pleased that going around these different characters holds
an audience; it's really the dramatic thread of the film. So from that
point of view it was a great film to do, although I was very nervous
making it and had a completely inexperienced crew.

*You worked with producer Kahane Corn and cinematographer Paul
Kloss.*
I'd not worked with them before and had really no money to make the

film, which was a co-production deal between, amongst others, BBC2 and HBO. What I tend to do is film for a very long time and put all the budget into the length of the shoot and then recoup from the back end. But because the shoot was so long, I couldn't afford a very experienced crew. Paul had just come out of the Austin, Texas, film school and hadn't really shot very much before and certainly hadn't shot very much in my style. Kahane, who was an extremely organized person, also had not worked my way before and had to get used to driving this enormous crew Cadillac around Los Angeles. I think it was harder for Paul because he wasn't used to working at the speed we were working at. By that I mean that one minute you would be sitting around and doing nothing and the next you would suddenly be filming. When you start filming everything needs to be immediately in focus, all the pans need to work, and Paul simply didn't know the equipment well enough. I ended up having literally to put him in a room when we weren't filming and get him to practice panning and focusing on objects without running film. I had to be quite tough on him but by the end he was shooting really well – though this initially created quite a lot of tension. I was nervous during the interviews and would have to tap Paul when I wanted him to pan. This was really tough on him but it was the only way of getting through the film. It wasn't exactly a love fest for either of us.

It was also a hard film to make because, for quite a long time, nobody would talk to us. I then realized that there was another English guy trying to make a film out there, a guy called Paul Buller, whom I'd initially contacted because we had a mutual friend. I'd told him that I intended to do this film and was very open because I had always been helped by other film-makers and journalists and have always tried to reciprocate. Unbeknownst to me, Paul literally went around and told Madam Alex that she would be nuts to do an interview with me and would be foolish to trust me. I also learned that the BBC person out in LA had done a very similar thing. I don't know exactly why. I think that Paul's proposed film was about the LAPD vice squad and Madam Alex was a character in it, so there was a very slight overlap of characters, but they were very different films. When I eventually got Madam Alex to take part in the film, she disclosed that Paul had advised her not to trust me, but she then demanded to be paid between three and five thousand dollars for the first interview, so there was a lot of debate over that. You have to be so persistent, otherwise you just do nothing. A time bomb is ticking because you are paying all these crew members but you aren't shooting anything; there is nothing worse. The tension was building, so in the end I had to offer Madam Alex what she wanted.

This becomes one of the motifs of the film, people counting out the money you have paid them to be interviewed. This indicates to me the level of morality these people operate at. Even Daryl Gates pockets $2,500.
That is very true of the first Aileen Wuornos film too. In this instance I decided to film it all because I thought that it was so much a part of LA and the way in which everybody valued themselves on what they were worth for the interview. Heidi Fleiss wanted even more money and ultimately Madam Alex got really pissed off with me because Heidi delighted in telling Madam Alex that she had been paid more money than her.

How much was Heidi paid?
I think she was paid $10,000. That was a good deal of the budget, but it was either pay these people or not get any footage. It was very much a part of the film and I felt so ridiculous, and then I was attacked in the

Madam Alex, *Heidi Fleiss: Hollywood Madam*

media for paying my subjects, which didn't make sense because it was one of the main structuring devices of the film. The point was that everybody had their price. People took this very purist idea that in documentaries you don't pay anyone.

Just out of interest, what would happen if with someone like Madam Alex you met her financial demands but then the interview was dreadful and she didn't disclose any interesting information? How would you handle such a situation?

I had a problem with Victoria Sellers,4 who was just telling me a load of crap, and I remember stopping the camera part way through and telling her that what she was saying was rubbish. She was high on drugs, but I had to make it clear to her that I expected her to tell me the truth. I do think that Victoria was pretty much out of control but after our little chat she was a little bit better. I didn't threaten not to pay her, as I didn't think that approach would work. It was a strange situation because all the other American tabloids were going around and paying these people as well, so it was a bit of a feeding frenzy. The tabloids expected Heidi and Madam Alex and all these girls to give the names of film stars who had been using their services and, although I wasn't interested in getting these names, it was all very much a part of this world. I felt that what *Heidi Fleiss* was doing was taking what was essentially a very tabloid story but explaining the background to it. I don't reveal a single name that you didn't already know about but was much more interested in showing who these people are, how they think, what their worlds are like, what their relationships are like and the kinds of dreams they aspire to. I literally did a non-fiction portrait of that world that was as accurate as possible in a way that a Raymond Chandler novel might have done it. I don't feel in any way that *Heidi Fleiss* is a tabloid film; a lot of people who wrote about it – some of them without having actually seen it – made the mistake of assuming that it was a tabloid muck-raking exercise. If somebody was to go and see it for that reason I think that they would be very disappointed.

Let's talk a bit about Ivan Nagy. At one point he asks you if he looks like he needs money and in the next moment proceeds to try to sell you a VHS tape of Heidi for $500.

Ivan was an interesting character because he had originally been a film

Ivan Nagy, *Heidi Fleiss: Hollywood Madam*

student of Colin Young at UCLA. When I started the film I rang Colin and asked him if he knew Ivan Nagy, and he told me that he was one of his more talented students. Ivan ended up making pornographic DVD features5 and has his own soft-porn business; he started off as quite a talented student but Los Angeles is a place where people incrementally change. I'm sure Ivan still thought that he was the same person, but he had become a real sleazebag.

You become quite confrontational with Ivan, asking him if he thinks the way he is living his life and living off Heidi is acceptable. I can't help but feel that this was a film that you became very personally involved in.
I think all the films are a search for a truth, whatever that truth may be, and I believed ultimately more in Heidi than I did in Ivan. Heidi is a very charismatic person and I liked her very much. Right from the beginning there was an odd friendship between Heidi and I – but I hasten to add that it was not a sexual friendship. I don't think Heidi is actually a very sexual person. I think she would agree that she is known in the city as the queen of sex, but she is unsure as to what all the fuss is about. To a certain extent, one always falls in love with one's subject.

But not Margaret Thatcher . . .
Well, maybe if I'd got closer to her . . . but you do get very involved in people's lives. In *The Leader, His Driver* I became very involved with JP and Anita. I wasn't actually in love with them but I cared and was involved. And I certainly liked hanging out with Heidi because she was enormous fun. Heidi had this funny little shop in Pasadena selling sweatshirts and T-shirts. I also felt that all the secrets were with her, that she was the one who knew what was going on. In a way one was drawn to that.

She strings you along though before she agrees to be filmed. Which reminds me of that moment where you go to her shop and Heidi asks another TV crew if she should be filmed by you, and the crew's attitude is, 'Well, who is he?' It amused me that you became so indignant at this.
The interviewer from this American TV crew was very opportunistic and out for herself, which is typical LA too. If in LA you are not from one of the recognized networks and you don't have your little badge and your little number and your Mercedes outside, then you are just not part of the club. I was in my lumberjack shirt and looking a mess with my raggedy crew and shooting on film – which nobody else was shooting on – and her attitude was, 'Who the fuck are you? This is our turf.'

That's why I feel that the kind of films I do are so necessary in America, because nobody is looking at the questions behind. They are all doing the ostensible surface thing – either news reports or celebrity titbits. It's all on a very mundane level and never goes into why something has happened.

Did that mean that your subjects were surprised when you began to ask more searching questions than they were perhaps used to?
Maybe initially, but then I think they were probably quite interested in getting into that. Both Ivan and Heidi were lying. This was an obsessive and very destructive relationship between them. Ivan and Madam Alex had also ganged up together and ratted on Heidi, which is why she was arrested. Heidi had then got Ivan arrested by saying that he was smuggling drugs into the country. The only way of understanding it was by realizing that the two of them were having this obsessive love affair that was still continuing. It was just the sickest thing. They

would say terrible things about each other to the press, do all these awful things and then fuck each other in the afternoon; they couldn't finish the relationship off. It's all there in that repulsive moment where Ivan insists on ringing Heidi up at the store to prove to me that they are still seeing each other. As a film-maker you had to be very involved with them, and I remember Kahane and Paul thinking I had lost my mind when I suggested that they were still seeing each other.

What did you think of the way Heidi was treated?
It's how that underworld operates. People are very much out for themselves and so without batting an eyelid will turn on the person who is down. I don't think that these are people who have examined life and said to themselves, 'How can I most enjoy life and what do I want from life?' They often find themselves in situations that they are unable to get out of and are frequently out of their mind on drugs. Madam Alex was taking pocketfuls of coke and would sometimes resemble a skunk because she would wipe the hand that she sniffed the coke with up through her hair, leaving a white streak. Ivan was taking uppers and downers, and Cookie was involved in the ecstasy thing. Heidi was on crystal meth, as were many of the girls who worked for her. As soon as you are dealing with people who are in a different reality by virtue of the drugs they are taking then none of the normal rules of conduct apply. People would get lost in their worlds – and the worlds of prostitutes and small-time crooks revolve around drugs and drink.

You show how this world also spreads to encompass the LAPD, something you also do in Biggie and Tupac. *There's no real governing justice system since the LAPD are turning a blind eye whilst these madams provide them with valuable information and other services. Heidi is persecuted by the LAPD because they claim that she is a poor informant.*
The unwritten understanding was that as long as you were useful to the LAPD, they wouldn't prosecute. As long as you were providing lists of clients and information about crimes that you knew about, then the LAPD would tolerate you. This was something that was very much set up under Daryl Gates. Mike Brambles, who was eventually arrested for rape and various other crimes of his own, was in charge of the west-side division and was Madam Alex's main contact point.

Being from a middle-class background I think it was difficult for Heidi to really understand those rules, that this was a serious game with hardball players, and she came unstuck because of it.

There was great surprise at the severity of her sentence and the general treatment she receives. Even one of the jurors, who accepts that she is guilty, expresses shock.
I remember talking to the district attorney and he felt that Heidi had been negligent with some of her girls and had allowed them to have sexual sessions with some unsavoury people, such as the Hollywood producer Don Simpson, who would allegedly beat and tie the girls up. I think that Victoria Sellers, whose relationship with Heidi was of the love–hate variety, had said something to the FBI out of pure vengeance after Heidi had thrown her out of her house. This made it appear as if Heidi didn't care about her girls and was quite happy to send them out into dangerous situations where they would get beaten up. There was a feeling that Heidi was duplicitous and evil, but this is certainly not something that I felt.

Heidi obviously has a self-destructive side to her and this seems to run in her family. Her sister is a heroin addict and there is something in Heidi that is drawn to having very abusive relationships with older guys. Most recently she was involved with actor Tom Sizemore, who abused her in an even worse way than Ivan. Bernie Cornfeld, one of Heidi's first older lovers, was probably quite kind to her. He was a sort of fun-loving and kindly crook, but there has subsequently been this string of mean, sleazy types. Who knows what it is in Heidi that attracts her to those people, but it is certainly a recurring thing. Heidi was also a very beautiful girl, but she then had all this awful cosmetic surgery done that destroyed the wonderful youthful look that she previously had. I found this really heartbreaking.

The final twenty-five minutes of the film are taken up with your interview with Heidi and you press her about her continuing relationship with Ivan. Did you not think that there was a danger that you were becoming too personally involved in Heidi's welfare?
No, but then I don't think I would have got the film that I did if I hadn't. You have to get really personally involved. As a film-maker you have to be careful that you get involved within the context of the existing relationships but don't become part of the relationship your-

self. This is something that you just cannot do. I don't do that in this film at all and haven't done it in any of the films. There is a definite line between having a close relationship with people and getting into their lives, their way of thinking and their trust without actually becoming somebody who changes their behaviour. My relationship with Ivan and Heidi was to find out what was happening. I think that the film had the effect of breaking their relationship up because after it was shown in Los Angeles it was just impossible for Heidi to be seen with Ivan any more after what she said. I remember showing Heidi the film, which I had to do before it came out, and the reason she was so upset with it was because it revealed that they had an ongoing relationship and she had to face that. She was horrified at the revelation that she was still seeing Ivan. At first she denied it, but later said that, if nothing else, the film stopped her from seeing him any more. She had even convinced her family and friends that she wasn't seeing Ivan any more and I think she detested herself for still seeing him, and yet that was the thing that drove her to see him still. It was totally perverse.

Is the fact that Heidi terminated the relationship one of the things that pleases you most about the film?
I think that it was a byproduct of the film. I feel that it is actually very much a film for me as I was living in LA. I was brought up in this very British way of believing that you do things in a proper manner and are rewarded for that. You know, you go into a meeting cleanly shaved, smartly dressed and making sense. You don't go in with your dress round your waist, half out of your mind and then emerge with a part in the film that you may have been auditioning for. But in LA that's exactly how it works. I was going out with an actress who would do exactly that; my proper public-school upbringing was thrown totally out the window. These were people who were involved with heads of studios and this was the way in which business was done. I didn't like this and feel very uncomfortable in that environment and don't view it as a desperately healthy way to conduct your life. For me it was a voyage of discovery. It was interesting and quite titillating to make, and I think that it is a very accurate portrait of that part of LA. For those reasons I am very proud of it. I also think that in some ways it moved a certain style along.

You have retained close relationships with some of the subjects of your

recent films. Is Heidi someone whom you are still in contact with?
She came to the première of *Aileen: The Life and Death of a Serial Killer*. Like myself, she is a friend of the record producer Rick Rubin, so we would often meet and go and have dinner at Rick's house. She's a friend and we chat on the phone. I've not spoken to her so much since I've been back in England but, in some ways, I think of her as a sister. Heidi is a very generous person and is very interested in people. She's also a great conversationalist and is very funny. She was very worried about my film initially, but I think it ended up being a very positive experience for her and she is now actually very proud of it.

Did you know that a fiction film starring Nicole Kidman as Heidi Fleiss has been mooted? It seems that all the films I've done are slowly being turned into features. Gus van Sant recently called me up and asked for some names as he's thinking of doing a film about Kurt Cobain.[6]

You seem to have a lot of fun with the sound effects on the film, especially in the early part where you show Heidi's growing up through a series of still photographs. For example, you show a still of Heidi scuba-diving and add the sound of bubbles to the image.
There was a lot of material. The secret of making these films is finding the material, so in this case it was finding the *Bobbit Uncut* footage and all the archival photograph material. This is a massive undertaking in and of itself, and then the trick becomes to incorporate it in the film in a creative and interesting way. It can really enhance a film, as it does in this case.

The way you use the archival family photographs with the veneer of normality on otherwise abnormal lives reminded me of Andrew Jarecki's Capturing the Friedmans *(2003).*
The *Heidi Fleiss* film is one that I think Andrew Jarecki admired. It is important to give a portrait of where someone's come from to get a little bit of their history. Still photographs are incredibly useful for that and are very revealing. They can be moving but also quite funny. People tend to take pictures of moments they want to remember, so you get a sense of people existing in a time when everything was all right. The flipside is also that nostalgia does have a tendency to be incredibly painful. You may look at a photograph of a relationship that might have ended and wonder if you couldn't have made it work

or made it go in a different way. As with most things, there is generally a sense of regret when looking at photographs. It can be even worse with film footage. Imagine how I feel when I look back at my older films and see how I've aged!

Shot inside Pandora's Box, a luxurious S&M parlour in downtown Manhattan, Fetishes *explores in a humorous manner a full range of fetishes, from rubber to infantilism, from asphyxiation to mummification. Revealing through the device of inter-title cards the historical background to sexual fetishes as well as some famous fetishists, including Mozart and Lawrence of Arabia, Broomfield's film – in which he takes a less conspicuous role than in some of his other works – also looks at the socio-political implications of a number of the clients' peccadilloes.*

The opening credits on Fetishes *tell us that the film was presented as part of the* America Undercover *series. What was that exactly?*
I was commissioned to do it by HBO as part of their series about schools, etc. My film was originally going to be in their *Real Sex* series, where they wanted me to do more of a travelogue of houses of domination or submission. The travelogue was to include New York, San Francisco, Los Angeles, Japan and England. I started researching it but a lot of the establishments were pretty depressing, so I thought that rather than doing an encyclopaedia it would be much more interesting to find one place and get into the characters and also really understand that world of fetishism.

I shot several different kinds of films really: I shot a film that was much more a portrait of Mistress Raven and the other women, and of Mistress Raven's relationship with her husband and all the shit that went down at Pandora's Box. Then I also shot the film that we see, which is much more of a portrait of the specific fetishes intended to act as an introduction to that world. I found that with more of a character study, something similar to *Chicken Ranch*, it became very difficult to get into any of the fetishes because when I got into a narrative story with the particular characters it became difficult to leave these characters to then spend five or six minutes on a fetish session. And so, to a certain extent, I sacrificed the characters' stories and told whatever was happening through the fetishes themselves.

I'm not sure that *Fetishes* is a film that I would have made by choice

Delilah and 'client', *Fetishes*

Mummification. Cinomatographer Christope Lanzenberg is in the background, *Fetishes*

under different circumstances. I'd just finished *Heidi Fleiss: Hollywood Madam* and I was totally broke when the commission came through from HBO. I thought that if I can't find a way of making it work then I won't do it, but whilst on a research trip I came across Pandora's Box and decided that I could do a film that would be worthwhile doing. Frankly, *Heidi Fleiss* became a commercial disaster and it shouldn't have been, but because it was an international co-production each partner wanted different formats and different versions. It was a complete nightmare. There were also distribution issues when the distributor suddenly demanded 10 per cent of the co-production finance, so I wasn't even able to pay myself a salary for that film. That said, I've never made a film that I haven't wanted to do and I really believed in *Fetishes* and it did become something that I felt accurately captured that world and that lifestyle and made it more accessible to people who may have previously been quite judgemental about it.

I like the way you set the fetishes out with the antique lettering on the inter-titles to give a brief explanation of each.
I thought those worked quite well. They were mainly used because in the first cut that I did of the film I had pretty much cut myself out

entirely, but then HBO felt that because it was quite an extreme subject the audience needed somebody to take them through it, a voice
to steer one through. I thought they were probably right. Again, like
Chicken Ranch, it could have been an observational piece, but I
ended up making it quirkier and putting myself and my narrative
into it.

*Your opening voice-over reveals that you were intrigued but uneasy
about fetishes. How much did you personally learn during the making
of the film?*
I'm not really into fetishes myself, though I have had relationships
with women who were and thoroughly enjoyed them. My appetites
are pretty unexceptional and this seemed to be a very specific world. It
really is a lifestyle and within these clubs there are all these people who
associate with each other and have their own specific language and
understandings and ways of behaving. I didn't know too much about
this and, if I'm honest, I did feel slightly uneasy. These places would
not be my environment of preference and it is hard when you are
walking around somewhere like the vault and there is some guy jerk-
ing off in the middle of the room. It does make one feel a little uneasy.
Many of the buildings are just very unappealing breeze-block con-
structions; it was slightly distressing to go into some of the houses of
submission to find all these young women in frilly nightdresses who
had been beaten black and blue by their clients. A lot of the girls working in some of the places I visited were very disturbed and at that point
I actually felt that I wasn't going to be able to do the film; it was just
too sad and there was nothing that fired my imagination or made me
feel good about the project. I hope that *Fetishes*, the film that I eventually made, is more of a celebration of that world. I liked Pandora's
Box because it was so beautifully done. It was like a Disneyland of
fetishes and one of those fantastic old brothels that you hear about in
Paris with their elegant theme rooms.

You also start with some archive footage that reminded me of The
Good Old Naughty Days *(2003)7 but also served a historical function:
to remind the spectator that fetishism has been around quite some
time.*
That was part of my own naivety. I had no real idea about the subject
and I was fascinated to learn that a lot of very famous and creative

people from the ancient Greeks through to Mozart had been fetishists. For a lot of people, when they see people with piercings it's a modern phenomenon, but it is a form of expression that has always gone on but society has always been quite dismissive and judgemental about it. What I wanted to try and do was make a film that was going to be for a mass audience and probably one of the first to be transmitted. There was the film by Beeban Kidron, *Hookers, Hustlers, Pimps and their Johns* (1993) that had been shown, but apart from that, there hadn't been that much.

You bring a lot of quite disparate elements together in this film. As we've already noted there are the inter-titles, the archive footage and your voice-over to guide the viewer, and there is also use of footage

Mistress Catherine and 'client', *Fetishes*

shot from a security camera, the speed of which you manipulate on
one occasion.

What was interesting about the film was that it was very depressing at
a certain length. The tone of the film really changed when I tightened
it and put the music in. When the sequences were longer, without any
effects, they were no longer funny or charming; they were just depressing and quite grotesque and ghastly. *Fetishes* certainly took a long time
in the editing room because I wanted to make something that an audience could sit through without getting upset or walking out. I was
making the film much more for an audience that was in the middle, as
opposed to the hard-core audience who was into the lifestyle. The tone
had to remain light, and I think those cards and the music helped that.
The film was also beautifully lit and shot by Christophe Lanzenberg,
who was more of a commercials DP than anything else, though he had
also shot the Madonna film *Truth or Dare* (1991).

Your cameramen always suffer on the shoots and Christophe gets bit-
ten by a lizard. One shouldn't laugh, but he gets bitten right after the
female owner tells you that it doesn't bite.

The lizard later bit off her nose. It was Christophe's idea to use the
CCTV footage. There was a camera to record people going in and
coming out, and I wanted to get a sense that there was a lot of other
activity going on, as we obviously couldn't film everything that was
happening there. I wanted to get a sense that within Pandora's Box
there were all these different doors to different rooms behind which
people were doing all kinds of different things. I also wanted to look
at the interchange between people, with the mistresses changing into
different gear for a session and clients sometimes being brought out of
a door and paraded around naked on a dog chain for the purposes of
public humiliation. The CCTV footage was a good way of compacting
all that stuff. It also gave it a truly voyeuristic feel.

Christophe very beautifully pre-lit the whole place before we started the shoot. He was also very beautiful and extremely popular with
the mistresses, which was extremely useful. He is a gourmet and every
night he would bring food into Pandora's Box and we would all eat
together. It helped to make us much more popular.

You talked about many of the other fetish emporiums you visited
being depressing, but when you interview the women who work at

Pandora's Box at their various apartments they seem to be living in comfort and appear to be relatively well off financially. They also seem to be quite empowered and fully in control of the men who visit them.
That's the idea, that the women come out of it empowered. Obviously the contradiction is that the men are paying, so ultimately the piper calls the tune. A number of the mistresses really were dominant women and I think it did empower them and fulfill some need they had to express themselves in this way. Obviously there were a couple of women who were into it just to make a living and it wasn't much of an expression of the empowering of their female self, but for some of them it certainly was and that's why it was much less depressing than the places of submission.

It's also interesting that two or three of the women trace their desire to dominate men back to their childhood. Similarly, one of the women who visits Pandora's Box and pays to be smacked discloses that this also harks back to her childhood.
I wanted to try and relate it back to something that would make sense. I think that most of these things go back to childhood and how we have been conditioned and what we expect and a lot of it is role-playing. The idea is that it is therapeutic and liberating. That may be true. A lot of the time one holds oneself so correctly; we are so restrained in terms of what we do that sometimes it is liberating just to let go and go into those hidden areas of our psyches and for that to be OK. You could be whoever you wanted to be and would be accepted on that basis in an unquestioning way.

Most of the mistresses who work there suggest that they get their own personal enjoyment from the sessions that they conduct where the client is female. You also make it clear that many of the women are bisexual.
A lot of the women had a very open sexuality and all the traditional sexual boundaries had gone. For them their sexuality was a complete expression and there was no limit to what they would try out and do. That's what that world was about really. I sometimes had a sense that there was this long dark tunnel and was unsure as to whether there ever would be any light at the end of it but the point was just to go as deep as possible into this world. There were some very hardcore characters there and occasionally one wonders whether a good straightforward session with a Freudian psychiatrist might not have been

more helpful. I think the guy who was talking about genocide and had his head down the toilet needed some pretty serious help.

The film shows the more straightforward fetishes such as submission, domination and suffocation, but some of the clients' particular sexual peccadilloes have far more disturbing social and political aspects to them. There's a black man who acts out the fantasy of being a planta- tion slave or the guy who has Holocaust fantasies.
They are very dark and, in fact, Mistress Raven tried to stop us from filming some of those. She did try to control the film for a while and ensure that we only included the more straightforward sessions. Indeed, there are fetishes that involve acting out some of the traumas that people have, and acting them out in their fantasies is just their way of releasing them. It is just their way of releasing them. For a lot of black clients, it was very much dealing with the black issue and being black in what was still a very racist society. I suppose that acting out the fantasy of being a plantation slave is a way of releasing one's own worst day-to-day feelings. We also filmed a very upsetting fanta- sy session that unfolded in a concentration camp where the Jewish client was selected as the one that the camp commander would have sex with. It was a quite formidable mistress that played the comman- der and part of it involved the placing of this guy's penis in a guillo- tine. The client just completely lost it and broke down sobbing. We had to stop filming. Apparently this 'meltdown' was quite a common occurrence.

Although concerned with issues of power and humiliation, there is very little sense that actual sexual intercourse went on.
I don't think it did, or very little, and it was certainly against the rules of the establishment. There was masturbation and that sort of thing. But though intercourse may have gone on, it certainly wasn't supposed to.

It's a very well-run operation. The safety of the girls does appear to be of paramount importance and there is a general concern for well- being. For example, the guy who has the Holocaust fantasies is vetted to make sure that he is not an anti-Semite who may then continue his fantasies outside of the confines of the establishment.
It was certainly one of the better run places and was amongst the pre-

mier establishments in New York. They had the top girls and clients from Wall Street. It was certainly very expensive.

The more debased the fetish, the higher earning and more high powered the individual it would seem.
They could indulge their fantasies more because they could afford it.

Alongside Soldier Girls – *which is arguably also about the men – and* Chicken Ranch, Fetishes *does seem to me to continue your fascination with the relationship between women and men, women and power, and women and sex.*
I have always been more interested in women who aren't the kind of county beauties who go straight into marriage. I have always been interested in looking at women who have challenged the accepted way of doing things or are outlaws in some way. This can't be applied so much to *Soldier Girls*, but it certainly applies to *Chicken Ranch* and *Fetishes* in terms of women who have moved away from the way that they have been brought up.

How did you win Mistress Raven and the other women over in terms of persuading them to allow you to film? And were the clients equally happy to be captured on camera?
I think at first that Mistress Raven was obstructive. This is not surprising given that she is a dominatrix and wants to control everything. There's a natural problem when you have a director who wants to control everything. Behind our backs Mistress Raven would try to give instructions to the girls in regard to what we could and couldn't do. In a sense we had to find girls who were more loyal to us than they were to Mistress Raven. Also, as the shoot wore on it became more difficult for Mistress Raven to be around all the time because we were putting in enormous hours and she would generally leave at around eight or nine o'clock at night. The clients would then often get thrown out because all the girls were having such a good time. A lot of the people we were working with there came to enjoy our company and realized that not only were we not sleazy, but that we were also quite good fun.

They give you a bit of a beating on your last day. You look genuinely afraid.
I knew that Mistress Raven really wanted to give me a session. She was desperate to tie me up and give me a good beating.

I can't imagine she's alone. Quite a few people in your films have wanted to do that and I'm sure that she could have got Eugene Terre'Blanche to join her.

She so wanted to give me a session and I wasn't going to let her. Maybe I'm a bit of a coward but I don't like losing control at all. Also, if I'd had a session, it would have changed my relationship with the other women there and I would have become too much of a participant. You just can't do that in a film. There's too much riding on it and you would just fuck the whole thing up if you stepped over that line. At least that was my excuse and I'm sticking to it.

That kind of goes both ways, though. In Fetishes *there's that disastrous wrestling match that threatens to spiral out of control and the mistress involved really shouts at you for not helping her when she was suffering. Should you not have intervened?*

It was certainly an ugly situation and I think that we were partly responsible for it. The problem was that I haven't had a lot of experience of these situations and it is always easy to be wise after the event. The guy thought that it was proper wrestling and was actually wrestling to win, whereas the mistress thought that it was role play and just a wrestling fetish. But being a dominatrix she wasn't going to let him win and at one point either bit or scratched him, and he considered this unsporting and went crazy. It was a mistake but this particularl mistress trusted us less afterwards.

And which women do you feel that you had the best relationships with?

I think probably Natasha, Beatrice, Delilah and Catherine – and, to an extent, Mistress Raven. Mistress Raven was very sweet but very difficult to deal with. Just before we started filming her lawyers called up and told us that we couldn't film. There was always about to be a problem. Her husband Richard, who is not in the finished film, was also a very complicated character. The first cut, the character study, had Richard in it and dealt with the contradictions of their relationship.

On most films I will do ten or more cuts that are fairly substantially different from one another, and the first versions of *Fetishes* were entirely different to the finished film. They hardly had me in them for a start and, as I've said, were much more of a character study. There were also some real fights between Richard and different girls and between Richard and us, and the first version of the film dealt with that. But then I felt that it should be mainly about the fetishes and how these fetishes came about as opposed to being just a study about these slightly eccentric individuals.

Do you also solicit the opinions of people whom you trust in regard to the edit that you should go with?
I do. I show them to different groups of people. Sometimes just by sitting with an audience you get a real sense of what works and what doesn't. Words don't even always need to be said. You can tell by the silence. You develop an extrasensory sense of communication in a semi-dark room and you know when a scene is working, just as you know when you want to crawl under the seat because a scene is so off. When you are editing, you tend to look at scenes in isolation; it's very rare that you really watch that scene in relation to the entire film, which is what you do in a screening where you see everything play out and are able to consider the relationship between one scene and another. I think that screenings are really important and they save a lot of time. It's a part of the process that can be the most interesting because you are trying to communicate ideas and it's interesting to see which ideas are communicated and which ones aren't.

When Fetishes *screened on British television, it wasn't met with outrage, but it was something of a 'water-cooler moment'.*
Michael Grade didn't want to buy it. He said they'd done their film on fetishes; that was the Beeban Kidron piece. Then Michael Grade left and Michael Jackson joined, and he bought it. It got very high ratings, but I didn't feel that there was enough discussion around it. It was just sort of put out there. I do remember that Kirby Dick was very annoyed with the film because it came out in America just before his own *Sick: The Life and Death of Bob Flanagan, Supermasochist* (1997) and he accused it of dampening the appetite for his film. I thought that this was unfair as his film was much more hardcore and really went into the whole fetish lifestyle.

What did Mistress Raven think of the finished film? Did she threaten you with another session?
The reaction was more from her husband Richard, who felt that it should have been more erotic. I thought it was quite erotic, and maybe

the mistresses didn't go into the more sexual stuff for fear that they would have problems with the licensing authorities.

Notes

1. Formally signed on 17 February 1986, Al Yamamah was worth an estimated £5 billion at the time and included the sale of Tornado and Hawk aircraft. British Aerospace – now BAe Systems – was the main contractor. A second deal, Al Yamamah II, was signed on 5 July 1988 and involved up to fifty more BAe Tornados, up to sixty more Hawks, more than eighty military helicopters, and air bases. It was valued at not less than £10 billion. Mark Thatcher, who was involved in brokering the deal, is currently facing fifteen years in jail for his alleged part in a supposed coup in South Africa.

2. 'Irrespective of the subject matter, however, there is really only one topic in all these films, and that is Broomfield himself.' Penn, Jim, *Contemporary British and Irish Film Directors*, p.43.

3. *Dark Victory: Ronald Reagan, MCA, and the Mob*. Moldea, Dan E. (Viking Press, 1986).

4. The daughter of Peter Sellers and Britt Ekland, Victoria Sellers was for a time a close friend of Heidi Fleiss before cutting a deal with the authorities and informing of Heidi's high-class call-girl ring. Having battled with numerous addictions, Sellers is now attempting to pursue a career as an actress.

5. The director of numerous cult TV shows, including *Starsky and Hutch* and *CHiPS*, Ivan Nagy's soft-core credits include: *Midnight Lace* (1981), *Trailer Trash Teri* (1998) and *Touch Me* (2001).

6. Currently in post-production, *Last Days* will star Michael Pitt as a Kurt Cobain-type musician from Seattle.

7. Directed by Michel Reilhac, *The Good Old Naughty Days* (*Polissons et galipettes*) is a risqué compilation of early pornography.

6

Music and Murder

Kurt and Courtney, Biggie and Tupac

Kurt Cobain

Courtney Love confronted, *Kurt and Courtney*

Beginning as a documentary about the music of Kurt Cobain, his con-
temporaries and the environment that informed them, Kurt and
Courtney *took a different turn when Cobain's widow, Courtney Love,*
refused to license Broomfield any of Cobain's music and then actively
tried to halt the making of the film. Changing tack, the director began
to make a film about the First Amendment, the controlling nature of
corporate America and the various conspiracy theories concerning the
apparent suicide of Kurt Cobain.

JW: *My understanding is that originally you were going to make a film*
about the whole Seattle/Portland music scene.
NB: I originally wanted to make a film about Kurt Cobain, but one
that would focus very much on his music and how that music
expressed the sentiments and emotions of a whole generation. The
whole kind of grunge/punk movement was against the materialism
and flash of pop culture. The scene also developed from a particular
area of America that is quite insular and understated. Somehow the
music was a manifestation of that. This makes more sense when you
go up to the north-east and you see the people who live there. It's very
blue collar and protective of itself. Kurt Cobain gave a voice to those
people who weren't obviously beautiful and who weren't Mr and Mrs
Popular in class.

Do you think that this is the same with many important counter-culture
musical movements, for example, punk and hip-hop?
Yes. It empowers a lot of people and validates them, especially the outsiders. This is certainly true of Kurt Cobain and his music. Although

Kurt was beautiful, he was an outsider and didn't really fit into the community where he grew up. He grew up in Aberdeen, a logging town where most of the guys were big strapping football players and he was this rather effeminate looking guy who, as ex-girlfriend Tracy Miranda tells us in the film, had to wear all these layers of clothing to make him look less slight. So the original idea was to give expression to all that, this music movement in a specific area of America and its anti-capitalist ethos.

I started making the film and was interviewing musicians who had been influenced by Kurt's music and also musicians who had influenced Kurt's music too, people like Mudhoney, The Melvins and Napalm Beach. A lot of these people had retired to obscurity and were living on welfare and a good many of them were also on drugs. It was really interesting to see what had happened to people who had at some point sold out stadiums and performed to thousands of people, but now nobody knew them any more. But then, about three weeks into the shoot, I found that I couldn't license any of Kurt's music. The irony was that I wasn't that interested in Courtney at the beginning. There were all these horrible stories about Courtney on drugs, burning down people's houses in Portland and drowning a kitten in a bath, but I really wasn't interested in any of this and certainly never planned to include any of it as it struck me as being bitchy and irrelevant. Also, with a film I always think that once you start shooting you are committed. If the going gets tough, you have to carry on and somehow integrate all the problems you are having into the making of the film. I regard these films as a diary of the experience of making the film. When Courtney's lawyers, her music company and her agents, ICM, started undermining the film by actively calling up people and saying that they wouldn't license the music and warning them off doing interviews with me, I had no option but to integrate all this into the film. I was doing a deal with Showtime, who were going to be the American financiers of the film, and Showtime wanted to bring MTV in. MTV obviously had a relationship with Courtney and, when she objected to their being involved, they, as a sister company of Showtime, managed to persuade Showtime to pull out entirely, leaving me without an American financier.

This is something of a Driving Me Crazy *moment in the film because you actually show yourself taking the call from the guy who tells you that they are pulling the plug.*

That's right, and I was quite a long way down the line at that point. It was very disappointing. The film then began to chronicle the difficulties of actually doing something that corporate America doesn't approve of. Originally I'd gone to HBO to finance the film, but because they were tied up with Time Warner, who had a lot of the rights to Kurt's music, they were really wary of the film and stipulated that the film couldn't be in any way critical of Kurt Cobain or his world as they didn't want to tread on Time Warner's toes. We got a sense that because so much of the media in America is controlled by big corporations – who have very diverse activities such as music publishing, news gathering, etc. – then the news and the information tends to get watered down because they don't want to be transgressing their other interests.

Originally, when the film was going to be shown at Sundance, Fine Line and Miramax wanted to buy the film. Fine Line are part of Viacom, and Viacom also own MTV and Showtime, so as soon as the shit started hitting the fan in Sundance they just walked away. A friend of mine was the head of acquisitions at Miramax and he received phone calls from ICM saying if you buy *Kurt and Courtney*, then you can forget having *x* number of stars in your next movie. The film and its release became an exploration of how difficult it is to put anything out in America today that corporate America does not approve of. There was incredible pressure applied to every distributor in an effort to persuade them not to buy the film. It was only because of The Roxy, this tiny distributor who also happened to own a cinema in San Francisco, that we managed to put it out. Right up to the release, The Roxy received hundreds of phone calls from ICM, the Kurt Cobain estate, Courtney's lawyers and countless other sources who were also targeting the radio stations and the journalists on the newspapers threatening legal action. Most people were frightened of it. Even my agents, William Morris, wouldn't allow the film to be shown on their premises for fear of legal action and reprisals from Courtney Love in terms of persuading the many music clients they represented to leave their stable. Cassian Elwes did an amazing job in showing it at Sundance but within the agency there was a very real fear of the film.

Was this personally debilitating?
It was, and if I hadn't had my lawyer Peter Dally, who really stuck by me at Sundance, I would have had a really hard time. The BBC, who

had put money into the film, went behind my back and their lawyer, Martyn Freeman, spoke to Sundance and told them not to reinstate the film. Martyn Freeman never told me or my commissioning editor at the BBC that he had done this. I later learned this fact from the Sundance Institute.

Can we just backtrack a little and talk about the whole Sundance episode. What actually happened?
I was on the jury there and *Kurt and Courtney* had also been selected to screen, but then, because of the various pressures, Sundance decided that they would be unable to screen it. Festival director Geoff Gilmore was really apologetic, but it's hard to know what really happened. I think that there was a certain amount of communication between Courtney Love and Robert Redford, and Pat Kingsley, the head of PMK and the publicist from hell, was both of their publicists. Although Redford was moderately two-faced about it, I don't think that he was supportive of the film. He made a big show of being filmed with me commiserating but what I gather from talking to other people is that Redford and the Sundance lawyer were on the side of the artist, the artist being Courtney Love. To tell you the truth, I don't think they even viewed my film.

I think Redford comes across very badly. The UK DVD of Kurt and Courtney *includes Redford's Sundance press conference explaining the decision to pull the film. On the one hand, he says that he believes in the right of freedom of speech, but then he goes on to explain that the film will not show and, to add insult to injury, gets your name wrong.*
That's right. I got a phone call from Page Four of the *New York Post* asking me why my film had been thrown out of the Sundance Film Festival. Sundance didn't even have the manners to call me directly and explain that they were taking this action; I received communication of this through the gossip columnists. After spending ages on the film, I was facing potential bankruptcy so I had no option but to wage war. Fortunately, because I was on the jury, I just took the film up there, did my jury duties and at the same time made sure that *Kurt and Courtney* had a special screening that was the highlight of the 1997 Sundance Festival. It screened at the Elks Lodge and sold out many times over, becoming the festival hot ticket.

Did the experience rekindle memories of the Juvenile Liaison *experience? I'm thinking especially in regard to the actions of the BBC over the film, a major British corporation again refusing to support you.*

It was exactly the same thing. My experience with institutions has been very bad. The trouble is that those kinds of institutions always have their own agenda and what's good for them goes first. I think that the BBC lawyers looking at *Kurt and Courtney* were far more worried about how the film reflected on the BBC than they were about my work and, once they realized that they might have a hard time from Courtney's lawyers, they seriously considered not putting it out. Worse, they tried to actually sell it to Courtney, but then realized that they didn't have the rights. Thirdly, they tried to bury it. Behind my back Martyn Freeman told Sundance to pull the film, and the thing that they pulled it over was actually the music footage that I'd licensed from the BBC itself. The footage was Nirvana performing on *Top of the Pops*; I'd paid £16,000 for it. The BBC release specifically stated world free TV and film festivals. This release was viewed and cleared by Martyn Freeman, who then accused me of not having got proper releases for it and charged me with being irresponsible. Because I was expecting something like this to happen, Peter Dally and I were really diligent and made sure that we got every single release that we had to get. The film that I presented at Sundance was absolutely fine to be screened and I felt incredibly betrayed by the BBC, the very people who should have been supporting me. All this came out of the blue to me in Sundance, where I felt like someone on the front line giving my life for this film. I felt very disempowered that all these things that were happening behind my back and that a force bigger than myself had taken control of the decision-making process. Sundance is supposed to be a celebration of independent film-making and was actually proving to be just the opposite. I was stuck in this motel in Sundance where none of the cell phones worked and I just felt absolutely besieged. It was a very lonely experience.

You had to resort to employing guerrilla tactics to get the film shown.

I had to do anything I could to get the film out there without recourse to the established way of doing things. To a certain extent, being an independent film-maker is being a guerrilla film-maker; you are trying to make it as cheaply as possible, bend rules, keep incidentals as small as possible, self-distribute, and all whilst trying to make a living off your project. When you are up against a lot of people with powerful lawyers who are used to getting their own way, you have to be very resourceful to stop them. It's not a good feeling really, but if you think that you have made something that is truthful and accurate and that you stand by then you just have to go the whole way with it.

The aftermath of the film was hideous, but you also described the shoot itself as being 'lots of druggy motels, bad meals and rain'.[1]
We had no money so we couldn't afford anywhere decent to stay, and once again I was working with ex-film students who didn't have any experience of shooting this way. One of them was very good, but the other didn't work out and I had to fire him. The whole thing was a bit of a mess and I was very much flying by the seat of my pants to see what I could make work. Also, a lot of the people whom I was trying to deal with were strung out on drugs and so were pretty unreliable and prone to lying and cheating. And the environment was pretty depressing, especially as we were there around the time of year that Kurt Cobain committed suicide and it was just days of rain and grey skies. I began to understand why people took so much crack up there. One is often up against it on these films and you just have to become quite tough to get through it. It's not particularly enjoyable and it doesn't always necessarily bring out the most sensitive and caring side of you.

You've also described the film as epochal.
It was, and then it just kind of burst at the end.

Joan Churchill worked on the film.
She came in part-way through. It was desperate times that threw us back together again. She was very kind to dig me out of the big hole that I was in and even did a deal with me whereby I could pay her a very small amount to carry on shooting. A number of the interviews had to be reshot because they were out of focus and technically not up to par.

Was that a nightmare situation, having to go back and reshoot interviews that you had already conducted?
In some of the cases I was clearer about what I wanted from the interview having watched the first one, but in other cases you don't quite

get the emotion that you have the first time. We just had to march through them but, on the whole, the second interviews actually worked out quite well. People also have a sense when you know what you are doing and when the camera is not moving all over the place.

Would you say that you don't tolerate fools when you are making these films? On a couple of occasions you have mentioned you have been forced to fire people part-way through shoots. You strike me as very single-minded.

I probably am. Shoots can be very frustrating experiences but things have to be done quickly and efficiently. Very little about film-making is to do with having a good time. Film-making is fascinating and interesting and often exhilarating, but shoots are very pressured and, with the type of films I make, there can often be this nagging sense that you are perhaps not getting all the information that you should and that there are stones that you may have left unturned. It is often these thoughts that lead you to finding something and having a breakthrough, but I personally have never achieved this by being very Zen. Maybe I should try it more, but it hasn't worked that way for me.

The film becomes a passionate crusade for freedom of speech, so one of the key moments of Kurt and Courtney *is when you take the stage at the ACLU awards[2] and address the guests about the contradiction of having Courtney Love as a guest, given her attempts to suppress not only your film but also the numerous violent threats she has made to other journalists. This has become a defining moment of your work, I feel.*

It was torturous to do as I am naturally a coward. It's a miracle I pulled it off, to be honest, as it was all about timing. I wasn't expected to take to the stage and had to just walk up in-between speakers. I was just fortunate enough to get to the lectern before the next person due to speak did.

You seemed composed.

Well, in a way I just went into automatic-pilot mode because I did know exactly what I was going to say. People were hissing at me and I was called a fucking idiot. Funnily enough, I was speaking to my agent the next day and he asked me if I'd heard about this fucking idiot who'd got up on the stage. When I told him it was me, I could

Nick takes to the stage at the ACLU awards,
Kurt and Courtney

hear him collapse onto his desk at the other end of the phone. Of
course, nobody really understood the relevance of my actions until the
film came out, but it does absolutely crystallize what the film is all
about. I did find it incredibly hard to do and it is a crowning moment,
but it certainly didn't come easily to me. I also had friends at the
ACLU gala who were begging me not to do it and who were literally
hiding under the tables when I went up.

*Unlike Al and Jack, the journalistic equivalent of paparazzi, you don't
lose your nerve when you do get up close to Courtney Love, asking her
about her threats toward journalists.*
You have to be prepared to ask difficult questions, otherwise you
might as well give up making the films. You have to believe in it
enough that you can justify your actions and just get on with it.

*The film became one that focused on Courtney Love, even though you
say that when you began making it you weren't particularly interested
in her. Did you attempt to speak with her?*

I tried really hard to talk to Courtney and went through every possible route. I even tried to get to her through her hairdresser and her make-up artist. She is an intimidating figure in so far as she has no reservations about punching people. This gave me a dilemma as regards what would I do if this woman attacks me? It's a lose/lose situation. I was anxious to avoid a physical confrontation. I was at a party and suddenly found myself dancing next to Courtney Love. I thought, 'Fucking hell,' but luckily she never realized.

Let's talk about some of the theories concerning Kurt Cobain's death that emerge in the film. Private Investigator Tom Grant is convinced that Cobain had been murdered. You say in the film that you don't believe these theories, but has anything come to light since to change your mind?

Nothing has come to light. There was a book written by Max Wallace[3] that trashes me for trashing the theory, the basis of the book. From Tom Grant's point of view, he was a private detective who was sitting in his office one Saturday morning when the phone rang. It was Courtney Love, who just happened to choose him out of the phone book with him just happening to be in his office. Courtney was at the Peninsula Hotel, running up and down the corridors strung out on drugs, and she commissioned him to go up to Seattle because I think she needed to be seen to be doing something about Kurt's whereabouts and his condition. It is very possible that she already knew that Kurt was dead. Tom Grant is dispatched to Seattle and is met by Dylan Carylson, who, as you saw from my film, is completely strung out on heroin. Dylan and Tom Grant go round the house, and I'm sure that Courtney imagined that they would check out the room above the garage and find the body, but that didn't happen. The body was, in fact, only found a few days later when Courtney employed an electrician to go and do some ostensible work. I think Courtney knew that Kurt was dead but she wanted someone else to discover him. Tom Grant became very suspicious of Courtney because of that.

I don't think that Courtney was particularly upset that Kurt was dead, and she stood to gain a lot from his death. There was nobody in Kurt's family that liked Courtney, but there simply wasn't the evidence to accuse Courtney of murder.

You have said that you don't wish Courtney any ill despite her actions, and in the film you actually speak in her defence when you interview her frankly repellent, self-serving father Hank Harrison.

At the point that I interviewed Hank – for what, I believe, was the third time and being very critical of him for his treatment of Courtney and the way he brought her up – the film could have gone in totally the opposite direction had I been able to get an interview with Courtney. One could have ended up with a more sympathetic understanding of her and the situation she had come to find herself in, but unfortunately that didn't happen. That was the film I expected to make. What actually happened was that Courtney just got more and more controlling; I think she only knows one gear and that is one driven by her will and fuelled by drugs. She would bludgeon people into accepting her opinion, which is also what she did with Kurt's friends when she sent a detective around to harass and intimidate them. Her actions left me with very few options but to make a film about that, and so that's what I ended up doing. I didn't actually want to make that film and it was an awful moment when I realized that I was going to be making a train-wreck film.

Hank's all about the money, isn't he? There's a very revealing moment where you turn up to interview him and he says, 'I see you've gotta better car. You must be making some money but I've not seen any of it.'

Hank really wanted fame and maybe that's where Courtney got a lot of her desire to be famous. There's a shamelessness about the pair of them that is ultimately self-destructive. Hank has this pretty plausible theory that the reason Courtney had so much facial surgery was to look less like him, and yet no matter what she does she is always going to be basically him and his spirit – which is a nightmare to think about. When you look at Courtney, you do get a feeling that she is trapped in this body that isn't her any more. It's quite ghastly. I feel very sad for her. Sometimes people tell me stories about her thinking that I will get some perverse enjoyment from hearing about her discomfort, and I absolutely don't. I have a real regret that things worked out the way they did. I think *Kurt and Courtney* is a portrait of a world and it lets you into that world and into that mentality. It really works in that way.

And did the film affect preserving the right to freedom of speech under

the first amendment? Did it lead to any sweeping changes?
No. Just look at America now. Freedom of the press is written into the constitution, but it is very hard to practise it when most of the newspaper, radio and TV stations are owned by such right-wing corporations, who owe their position very much to the Republicans and would do anything to avoid criticizing them. I think that extends to anything that threatens making money. The highest goal is to make money and anything that could affect that is not tolerated. Kurt Cobain, at this point in time, is a money-generating concept. Everything that he stood for is irrelevant to the record companies and the corporations that are making money from him and his songs. They don't want to face anything that could impact upon that. Kurt's music generates around $11 million per year so the loyalties of the record company are clearly with Courtney, the estate and that money – that's their thinking process. Until there are more independent outlets for films, writing and expression in America, there is going to be a real problem. Look at what happened when people tried to get accurate information about what was happening in Iraq or in Afghanistan, or, and even closer to home, what happened during the Florida election. They just don't get given this information and, increasingly, they don't seem to ask for it either. You get a sense of this enormous country with all the technological capabilities of disseminating information, yet only a very narrow amount of information is coming through.

So Kurt and Courtney *was a traumatic experience from start to finish, but how do you view the film in retrospect?*
It was a very painful film to make. Incidentally, how many of the films am I saying that about?

Almost all of them, actually.
Oh God. It was a desperate film and I thought that a lot of the subsequent battling in the media was unsightly and rather low-down and miserable. I felt that life was too short for all that and it certainly wasn't the way I wanted to live my life; it was bringing me into contact with a lot of ghastly people. It's a very extreme film about a very extreme situation and I think it mirrors that. In an odd way, I think that some of the way it was shot – the technical flaws that I was quite critical of at the time and which made it very difficult to edit – actually fits in and captures the craziness of the situations and of the people

we interviewed. I sometimes feel that I am half out of my mind on drugs when I am looking at it. I actually think it's a miracle that *Kurt and Courtne*y ever got released but I'm not sure that the film is really me; I got it done out of sheer stubbornness. It's so far removed from what I set out to make. I had visions of a celebration, but instead this is just a long, dark and deranged journey.

Biggie and Tupac, *an exploration into the murders of Tupac Shakur and Christopher Wallace, a.k.a. Biggie Smalls, two of America's biggest rap stars, uncovers the apparent collusion of both the LAPD – Broomfield interviews at length former LAPD detective Russell Poole – and Death Row records impresario Suge Knight. Examining from an historical perspective the uneasy relationship between the FBI and prominent black militant figures, Broomfield's film offers not only a gripping investigation into the slayings but also a telling depiction of an increasingly lucrative counter-culture and a clandestine, inherently racist justice system.*

Biggie and Tupac *is the second ostensibly music-themed film on the bounce after* Kurt and Courtney. *What initially interested you in making it?*

Biggie Smalls and Tupac Shakur, *Biggie and Tupac*

People kept asking me if I wanted to do a film about Biggie and Tupac, and I kept saying no. Michael Jackson at Channel Four called me up saying, 'Biggie and Tupac, Biggie and Tupac.' I'd be having a shave in the morning and the phone would ring, and it'd be Michael Jackson saying, 'I've been thinking again, have you changed your mind about doing Biggie and Tupac?' And I was like, 'NO', and he said, 'Well, let me know when you have.' This happened literally three or four times. I was trying to make all these other films, specifically a series on world leaders – Fidel Castro, Arafat, Gadaffi – and I wrote this major proposal to Channel Four.

Is this still something you'd still like to do?
I would still probably quite like to do it. I mean, obviously time moves on, but I thought it would have been a great series of films. I spent a whole summer researching them and Channel Four just wasn't interested in doing them. So I was persisting in doing those and Channel Four were then trying to get me to come in for meetings to commit to a film. I would go in there with Charles Finch, who represented me, and we'd have the most hilarious meetings and nothing was ever resolved. It sort of became a standing joke that we'd have all these meetings and consume vast quantities of food and alcohol and nothing would happen. Then Michele D'Acosta, whom I'd made *Fetishes* with, became really interested in finding out about Tupac Shakur. Michele was born to Jamaican parents but was adopted by a white family on the Sussex coast and was the only black girl in a hundred miles. For her, finding out about Tupac was a sort of pilgrimage to get back in touch with her roots.

Is that one of the things that persuaded you to do the film?
Well, she was very dedicated to working on that and I'd really enjoyed working with her. I thought she was very talented, very committed in her work; we would meet occasionally over the course of two or three years and she would tell me about the work she was doing with Tupac. Michele had gone back to Baltimore and made contact with his teachers. I think Tupac had also grown up around a lot of white people, especially at his school, the Baltimore School of the Arts, which was predominantly white and Jewish. He was talented enough to get in, had a very close relationship with a lot of white people, so there was always a sort of strange . . . I don't know how I'd put it, a sort of con-

Tupac Shakur and Afeni, his mother,
Biggie and Tupac

fusion of roles. And I think maybe later in life he became more hard-
core and started acting a role. And I think Michele very much identified with that.

And then there was the big Ramparts scandal in Los Angeles where
a number of LAPD police officers had been implicated in drugs, drug
running, money laundering, murder and so on in the Ramparts area,
which is an area of Los Angeles with a high number of immigrants.
There was an indication that some of the police officers were members

192

either of the Crips or the Bloods, the two main LA gangs, and I'd always wanted to do something about the LAPD, having lived in LA for a long time. The film seemed a way of investigating the police force as well as looking at the racial composition of LA and these two rap singers, Tupac Shakur and Biggie Smalls, who were singing about exactly the kind of subject matter the film was going to be about. It was this scandal that really persuaded me to do the film.

Did you initially feel a resistance because you were a white male making a film about a black culture?
I did, but I also think it was much worse in anticipation than when I actually got on with it. That was partly because most of my white friends who lived in LA had never been to Compton and Watts, had never been to the black areas of the city, and they were completely paranoid about them. When I said I was going to do this film, they immediately predicted hails of bullets going through my house and that I would be shot and somehow expose a lot of them to danger; that's the level of paranoia in America. And when you actually get to Watts and Compton, you find that people are incredibly hospitable and flattered that you are interested in being there. They couldn't be nicer to you and are much friendlier than anywhere else in LA. There'd been so much hardship down there and so much brutality, and when people in those communities realize that you are serious and committed to your work they couldn't be more co-operative. All those initial barriers go very, very quickly.

Were there any interviews that were difficult? An extra on the UK DVD of Biggie and Tupac *shows a very uncomfortable interview with Outlaw.*
That was with Tupac's backing group. Mopreme was also pretty difficult. Mopreme was Tupac's half-brother but had really been short-changed. He'd never really been helped by Tupac's mother Afeni and hadn't really had a very successful career as a rap artist. He was really broke and very resentful and embittered. He was a bit of a victim and had been quite badly beaten up by Suge Knight and was suspicious of me as a white boy making a film about rapping.

He's very profound. I was moved by his 'The way you judge a man's character is how he comes back from adversity' speech.

Mopreme (right) with his best friend. Mopreme was Tupac's
half brother, *Biggie and Tupac*

Our relationship was slightly humiliating too, as people like Mopreme
hope to be discovered as rap artists and, in a sense, their association
with Tupac was doubly painful not only because Tupac was murdered,
but also because he represented the success they had never had. The
few possessions of Tupac's that they retained – like his photographs or
little recordings they had of him jamming with them – they somehow
believed were going to be their ticket to either success, money or mainstream American culture. And, of course, a lot of their hopes were
really misplaced.

*There is that scene where you show a guy trying to play you a tape of
Tupac's early music and the tape doesn't work.*
And he doesn't actually have the rights to the music and faced being
sued by the record company. In the meantime, he was working as an
electrician in Baltimore. He was a really sweet guy with a family
who'd had a taste of fame and success with Tupac, so there was a lot
of confusion and disillusionment. A lot of that initial grandstanding
and appearing tough, if you gave it a moment you realized there was
a whole different scenario going on, and he was a really caring individual who'd had some bad experiences. There isn't one member of
that community who hasn't been arrested numerous times by the
police or been harassed or beaten up, either because they're black or

because they have some kind of loose association with gangs, an association which you can't avoid. If you don't belong to a gang or don't have some kind of affiliation with a gang in those neighbourhoods, you get killed or you get beaten up and are constantly picked on. It's very easy for us to take a negative position regarding gang membership, but the reality of living in those ghettos, which is really what they are, is that you have to take sides. That way you get protection.

In Heidi Fleiss: Hollywood Madam *you showed that the line between criminal activity and the police is blurred. Were even you surprised by some of the things that you uncovered in* Biggie and Tupac? *I was amazed by the idea that the FBI had since the forties carried out surveillance to monitor prominent hip-hop dealers who had been associated with the Black Panthers.*

I think that the FBI has never dropped the idea that any kind of organization among the black community could totally destabilize America. I think this is the paranoia of America. Actually, the country hasn't moved on that much since the civil rights movement. Until the mid-sixties, the blacks living in Watts and Compton couldn't even go to Santa Monica beach; there was a whole area, where the Magic Mountain is, where the blacks had to go for their holidays because they weren't allowed in the other areas. And they were only allowed to live in certain parts of the town. And, OK, that's sort of changed in theory, but because the black schools are still so bad and the economic opportunities in the black communities are still so limited they still tend to be in those areas – Compton and Watts, or whatever – and the normal white person in Los Angeles has very little interaction with them. Because of this, there is a split community. That's why during the LA riots there was a real panic that Beverly Hills and the rich areas of LA were going to be overwhelmed by this horde of black looters; this is symptomatic of a general fear throughout America that this is going to happen. So the FBI, from the Black Panthers on – and probably before the Black Panthers – has really closely monitored the black community. I think the FBI's biggest fear is that they will become organized on a political level, particularly with someone like Tupac, who indicated an interest in going into politics and was much more overtly political than Biggie and whose mother had Black Panther connections. They monitored him very closely.

It's interesting that members of the LAPD, such as Officers Gaines and Perez, were moonlighting for companies such as Death Row Records as bodyguards.

It's to do with this whole idea in the American psyche that things can be privatized, that policemen can work as security or bouncers to avail themselves of more money. This is done all over America. It's free enterprise and is highly approved of. The only trouble with Death Row Records is that it had criminal associations and there was a strong indication that they were involved with moving drugs around as well. The whole drug issue is very interesting and something I nearly went into in the film. There is evidence that the CIA was involved in drugs for arms during the Nicaraguan war, that they were funding the Contras, and those drugs were going through Compton and Watts and those black communities. The gangs were then used to distribute those drugs. In fact, Harry O, the founder of Death Row Records and its first major investor, was a gang figure convicted of dealing cocaine. He

LAPD Officer David Mack,
Biggie and Tupac

invested the money that he made from selling it into Suge Knight and the formation of Death Row Records.

What's also interesting about all this is that Death Row Records was a subsidiary of the white-owned Interscope Records. Interscope had money from Time Warner, so this is another example of corporate white America availing themselves of this incredible art form that had actually originated in Watts with The Watts Prophets.

With the information the film imparts on the background of Biggie and Tupac, the overview of the hip-hop movement and the Black Panthers, the LAPD, the different theories regarding the deaths of Biggie and Tupac – I would imagine that the research on this film must have been extremely extensive.
It was a very vast subject and the amount of research was gigantic. Michele D'Acosta and Barney did an amazing job going through stuff. We had the whole murder book to go through. There was a book by Ronin Ro called *Have Gun Will Travel: The Spectacular Rise and Violent Fall of Death Row Records*,[4] which is about Death Row Records and Suge Knight's reign of terror there. Unbelievably, Death Row Records was part of the same building as Interscope, with just a door separating the two. Occasionally, people with blood dripping out of their mouths who had just been beaten up would stagger into Interscope and the staff would pretend they didn't know what was going on.

It was as overt as that?
It was. And Suge Knight, having been someone who was in a prison, employed his old prison buddies, who were all members of the Bloods, to act as security for Death Row Records. That's how he ruled. These guys were just straightforward thugs who'd grown up in a history of violence and who'd run the drugs in Compton.

Your son Barney is one of the executive producers on this film. Was it exciting to work with him on this project and – to take up your point earlier about your getting ideas from him – was this the case here?
He and Michele are very close, and Michele has a very thorough way of working and a very detailed mind. I'm not a great researcher; I'm much too impatient and want everything immediately. Research doesn't work like that – you have to be very diligent. She and Barney really read a lot and would spend hours and hours theorizing on this,

Death Row Records insignia on Suge Knight's car
Biggie and Tupac

that and the other. Also, we had Russell Poole's work on the murder, a book that went literally from here to the floor. It was four foot high. Barney, at that time, was at Santa Cruz University and managed to persuade them to allow him to submit, as part of his second-year exams, a paper on the film. They subsequently allowed him to be absent for three or four months, submitting periodic papers. The working relationship actually started really badly because Barney was not used to working in this disciplined way. He's a night owl, so he would get up after we'd all been working for a couple of hours. He did sort of apply himself then, but making a film isn't really like that; you don't kind of get up when you want to you.

How did that resolve itself?
I had a bit of a showdown with him after a couple of weeks. I told him that I didn't think that it was working out and that he ought to go back to college as I didn't want to fight with him. It was pretty unpleasant, particularly as Joan Churchill was working on the film as well. The enterprise felt doomed and I was beginning to think that it was a mistake to involve so many people I am so close to; Michele was

a really close friend, as well. But Barney really changed then. He threw himself into the film and worked incredibly hard. We were all working from the house in Santa Monica, and Barney loves telling the story of how no one would ever come to visit the house after a while because we were all totally obsessed with this subject. We were completely unable to relate to anybody else and their lives for longer than two minutes. We'd find some way back into the subject, which must have been unbelievably boring for any friends who were dropping by for a cup of tea. And that's pretty much the way it was for three and a half months.

These things really take over your life to that extent?
Completely. We'd get into the regime of getting an hour of exercise a day and eating, sleeping and nothing else at all. And we were all more than ready to finish at the end. I think it would have been good to have had a bigger research team.

Have you ever been put in the position where somebody's brought you research that's been inaccurate?
A lot of it is based on summation. I mean, the whole theory that police officers were involved with Death Row Records has yet to be proved correct. The case brought against the LAPD for the wrongful death of Christopher Wallace, a.k.a. Biggie Smalls, was referred to a Superior Court judge on 21 June 2004, who allowed it to go forward on the basis that police radios were definitely used to co-ordinate the hit and that the LAPD had information about the exit that Christopher Wallace would be using from the Petersen Motor Museum.[5] Police radios were also used to facilitate the exit of the person who shot Christopher Wallace. And on that basis they've allowed the case to go forward, but it's still to be proved right. To a certain extent, as a film-maker, what you're doing is trying to evaluate how accurate you think the information is. Obviously you come across conspiracy theories that have got no merit at all.

And what about in this instance, because I think it's clear that the murder was set up by Death Row Records and then presented as an East Coast/West Coast feud between Biggie and Tupac.
Well, I think Death Row Records was basically a criminal organization set up with drug money, staffed by ex-cons and run by Suge

Knight, who definitely had very strong connections to the Bloods and gangs in Compton. Their whole modus operandi is one of violence. You look at Suge Knight's whole life and it's understandable because he grew up with the violence of Compton. He was surrounded by murders from a very early age and he, not surprisingly, perpetuated that. His life was a series of assaults and acts of violence, and I think this was just second nature. He seems to be obsessed with dominating his business ventures with that violence and he did that to people on the West Coast. He obviously enjoys beating people up and he was also into humiliating men and seeing them sodomized, so much a part of prison culture. He brought that into Death Row Records, and the tales of what he did to people meant that he was quite successful in business. If Suge Knight says, 'I want your music rights,' then you best let him have them. I mean, someone like P. Diddy, he wouldn't behave like that. He's just a businessman, and a very good one. I'm sure he gets up people's noses, but he's not someone who is going looking for a fight. He's interested in business machinations, not outgunning people and buggery. Suge Knight brought all that into the business.

Did Suge Knight also propagate the extent of the rift between Biggie and Tupac? They obviously had a falling out, but in the film you reveal that Biggie visited Tupac after he'd been shot the first time.
He exaggerated it, certainly. Biggie and Tupac were very similar in a way. Both of them were A-stream students at school and were very, very successful as academics and poets before they even got into doing hip-hop, and I think there was a real connection between the two of them. Tupac really helped Biggie and was therefore admired by him. But Biggie was obviously enormously humiliated when Tupac went off with his wife, Faith Adams.

Biggie came from a very loving background. There's the great story his mother Voletta tells about the time he wouldn't hang up the phone until she said that she loved him.
That is a very endearing story.

Tupac, however, seemed to be surrounded by people who didn't have his best interests at heart. His whole attitude and demeanour seemed to change, as evidenced by the footage you show of him spitting at journalists.

Tupac Strikes a pose, *Biggie and Tupac*

At the Baltimore School of Arts he was obviously really loved and a lot of his closest friends were white. In fact, there was even the suggestion of a sexual relationship with a couple of them; well, certainly with this guy he called White Boy John. Tupac was of slight build and he was quite effeminate and beautiful, and when he started hanging out with people like Suge Knight and all these convicts, who were all bloody enormous, frankly, he had a lot to prove. And I think that they weren't that respectful of Tupac. Their culture is all about who's the toughest, who's the strongest, who's the most macho. That's what prison culture is all about; it's about straightforward physical strength, and I think Tupac was kind of enamoured of that and he kind of respected that in an odd way. I think it really changed him. He wanted to be accepted by these people.

Let's talk about the interview with Suge Knight. When you interview him in prison he sends out all these positive messages to 'the kids', but when you subsequently log onto his website after his release there's a message sending out a death threat to Snoop Dogg!
That's right.

Was it an intimidating experience at Mule Creek Penitentiary?
It was, partly because the whole place was kind of nuts and out of control. Joan was very concerned because she lives in Los Angeles and didn't want to put her driver's licence number or address down in the prison logbook. I could put my British address, but in prison it's not too hard to get hold of this information, so Joan was understandably concerned about her safety. These concerns were increased by the fact that we were getting all these calls from Death Row Records about where we were staying and what flight we were on – seven or eight a day, all increasingly menacing. They were furious that we were going up to the penitentiary without taking one of them with us as I'd refused to put down a member of Death Row as part of my crew.

Would that have been Reggie Jr?
That was Reggie Jr.

He didn't like the Heidi Fleiss film, did he?
He didn't like the *Heidi Fleiss* film. 'You're not going to pull that Heidi Fleiss shit!'

The look on your face is priceless.
I was pretty surprised that he had seen the film.

So you go through all this and then your cameraman gets what you describe as an attack of the 'heebie-jeebies'.
Mark Strasberg was totally freaked out. It was when I was going up to Mule Creek that Joan decided not to come. She recommended Mark, who, she said, had just recently finished a film in a prison. And I took her on her word. As we were driving up I said, 'What's the film you did in the prison?' and it was a Walter Hill drama in a prison that was not only new but also had no prisoners in it. They were all actors. So Mark hadn't been in a real prison with real prisoners, but he felt that he would be able to cope with the atmosphere. Of course, when we got there it was fucking crazy, and there's me saying, 'Shoot everything,' and the warden is saying, 'Don't shoot this and don't shoot that.'

So you then become responsible for not only having to do these interviews but also making sure your cameraman is getting the footage you need.

Yeah, you get very worried about what's being covered and what isn't, and you see somebody who is panicking because they're over-whelmed. It's like going into a war zone with somebody who has never been under fire before. To expect them to carry it off is unrealistic. It was a very intense situation, but I think in a way it actually adds to the film because the audience is placed in the position of this poor cam-eraman who is beleaguered and doesn't know what to do. A lot of the tension in that scene comes from his frenetic camerawork. When I was first trying to cut it I was in despair because I tried to cut it properly and there were so few shots that were held steady for more than two seconds that it was almost impossible to edit. I tried so many times and then I thought, 'Oh well, I'm just going to go with it.' What's great about making these non-fiction films is that they are to do with what actually happened as against what you would like to happen or what you think should happen. And the more you adhere to that truth, the stronger they normally are. So once I built the cameraman's fear into the scene and constructed the scene around that, it worked very well. But it took a while to get to that point.

And what about the actual interview? Because I have to say, and this is probably a part of his charm, Suge Knight comes across as quite a nice chap.
He's very soft spoken. Suge is a massive guy who's got this very high-pitched, quite effeminate voice. Very soft spoken. I mean, you can hardly hear what he's saying. Although when he starts calling people 'snitches', then you realize that there's this other side. I think the man is actually like a volcano. He's capable of the most amazing violence and there's something really sadistic and very peculiar on a sexual level with Suge Knight. I think he's very fucked up, sexually, but I was strenuously warned not to ask him anything about his homosexuality or to ask him anything about buggery or that sort of thing.

And you decided to heed that advice on this occasion?
I felt that I wasn't going to do that sort of combative interview with Suge Knight. It would have been pretty foolish and, in a sense, it's important to remind oneself of that. It's not so much about Suge Knight being the big terrible guy. He is very much the victim in that he is so much the product of Compton, and if Suge Knight had grown up in a neighbour-hood that wasn't on the brink of civil war, that wasn't struggling for

Suge Knight and Tupac Shakur, *Biggie and Tupac*

every penny, where there wasn't this kind of drug dealing and violence, if he'd grown up in another kind of community where there was proper schooling and there were adequate jobs, I think he probably would have been a very different person. So I didn't want him to be the big bad guy that all our attention was focused on. Maybe I should have made more of a thing about Interscope though, and the fact that someone like Suge Knight was still working for 'whitey'.

I was interested by the fact that Russell Poole, who comes across as a very upstanding, honest man, is forbidden by his lawyers from speaking with you and initially gives you the run-around, but then he decides to meet with you against their advice.

He had that sense of honour and a sense of the way things should be. He was an idealist and a lot of his idealism came from his father. I think there's a slight hint of racism in Russell Poole, although he would not see it that way. I think what happened with the LAPD was that a predominantly white police force, made up mainly of former Marines, had evolved into paramilitary police force. It was very mechanized and was the first police force to use helicopters. It had the city all broken down with military precision into a grid plan so they knew what to do when trouble went down. In short, it was the opposite of community-relations policing. You could never reason with an LAPD police officer. Everything was pretty much done by the book.

Then, in the nineties, the LAPD were criticized for being segregationist and for the fact that there weren't enough black people being employed, and so a lot of black policemen were inducted very quickly. All the normal routine searches were kind of waived and a number of black officers were inducted into the force who had gang ties. I think Russell thought that these were people who shouldn't have been in the force and that its reputation was besmirched. And I think he was someone who would have supported Daryl Gates, who was the last white head of the LAPD. So there's that undercurrent, which I didn't really go into. But maybe that's what always happens in a country where you're trying to open things up and move things on.

And do you feel Poole was driven by a genuine sense of justice?
I think he absolutely believed in what he was doing. This is a man who, like a lot of whistleblowers, was driven into an extreme position and, in a sense, the LAPD wanted to drive him into an extreme position – possibly giving him a nervous breakdown – to devalue what he was saying and the accusations he was making. It's interesting that when ties between the LAPD and the death of Biggie Smalls began to appear, the LAPD claimed that if an officer such as David Mack was working for Death Row in his own private time, then he couldn't be accused of doing it under public law of the uniform. In other words, the LAPD won't accept any responsibility because they're saying that Mack was off-duty and was doing it as a private citizen rather than as a member of the LAPD. The whole thing goes very deep.

Kevin Hackie, the other ex-LAPD officer you interview, doesn't strike one as entirely trustworthy but he does identify Harry Billips, a.k.a.

Amir Muhammad, the man accused of carrying out the Biggie killing.
I think Hackie is a bit of a devious character who, again, is bitten by
the American dream. He wants to make a fortune. He wants a yacht,
he wants a good life, he wants the women and all the rest of it. And he
sees all these people who've got all that and thinks he should have it,
and he sees the information he has about the murder of Biggie Smalls
as his ticket to lots of money. He was always trying to sell me his information.

Did you pay him any money?
No. So he comes across as a bit of a devious guy, but I think he knew
a lot. Not as much as he was letting on; he's a bit of a con man. I think
he's very much representative of the need to succeed, the need to make
money. That's what has caused the corruption in the LAPD and probably the corruption in the hip-hop movement as well, and Hackie is
just an embodiment of all that.

*Biggie's mother Voletta emerges from the film as a wonderful, caring
person. She seems genuinely to welcome you into her home and into
her life, because she feels that you are making something worthwhile.*
Well, at first Voletta didn't want to talk to us. I had several conversations with her at first on the phone which were, 'Oh, I'll call you back.'
She was always very polite and always said, 'Well, I'll talk to you on
Monday,' and then I'd never hear from her. It was very difficult with
some of these people when you sense that person has real grief and
you're going to be getting them to talk about something very painful.
It's quite hard to be persistent and I think it was only at the point when
she realized that I was very serious about getting to the bottom of the
murders, that I had been in touch with Russell Poole, had the murder
book and we were talking to several people that she agreed to talk to
us. Voletta also became aware that this wasn't another of those puff
pieces that they show on MTV and understood that it was a serious
film. Once she agreed to talk to us, she was extremely co-operative
because more than anything she wanted to get to the bottom of the
murders. I think people like Faith Adams and Sean 'P. Diddy' Coombs
had turned their back on her and were moving on with their lives, feeling that Biggie's death was an unfortunate incident that they didn't
want to dwell on. For Voletta, it was very different as this was her life
and she needed to get some resolution and a sense of justice. One of

the most appalling aspects of the story is that everyone was just moving on and that Biggie and Tupac were just regarded as hoods and so not worthy of any resolution or justice.

As it concludes, Biggie and Tupac *brings together Voletta and Russell Poole, with Russell helping Voletta bring her wrongful death lawsuit against the LAPD for the death of her son. Even though the case is ongoing, is this a pleasing situation to have played a part in instigating?* It is, but I'll be happiest when we get to the bottom of these murders.

Do you think we ever will?

Russell Poole and Voletta Wallace sifting
through evidence, *Biggie and Tupac*

Well, there are definitely people out there who know what happened. I mean, there must be. And as long as those people are alive, there's a hope that someone will come forward. It just needs someone to come forward. I imagine that Reggie Jr must know everything.

And what about Harry Billips/Amir Muhammad, the man identified by several parties as being responsible for the Biggie murder?
I think Harry Billips has been under surveillance, but they haven't managed to get anything on him. Various pieces have also appeared in the *Los Angeles Times* casting doubt on Russell Poole's theory and the idea that Harry Billips is in any way responsible. I'll be delighted when it moves forward and something comes out of it. The thing that is important is that the American justice system is looked at or the internal mechanisms within the LAPD are looked at because they've done such a lousy job at following up on the investigation. Voletta is called once every six months by the officers who are supposedly investigating the case, but they just don't care. Also, and more malevolently, they have so much to lose by what might be revealed by the case.

Like Heidi Fleiss: Hollywood Madam *and, to an extent,* Kurt and Courtney, Biggie and Tupac *structurally resembles a detective story. Was this deliberate? I'm thinking of the brooding incidental music you use.*
It was because these films are diaries. A lot of the structure of the film is about the investigation and about the dead ends you come to. The film is also a portrait of that world, with its hearsay, speculation and the infighting between the various groups involved. It's quite interesting to get a feel of those things in the film as well.

Were there repercussions after the film's completion from people at Death Row Records?
No, because by the time the film came out, Suge Knight, who had been released in the interim, had been rearrested and was back in prison. But there was an amazing panic on the part of Lions Gate, who were originally going to be the distributors of the film. They got worried about lawsuits. There were also concerns about gang violence in the cinemas and, in fact, a lot of the cinema chains wouldn't take the film for fear of gunfights. Some of the cinemas actually insisted we hire security for each screening. This was just not practical and is evidence

of the heightened paranoia that I think America has concerning gang violence. Moreover, it almost made the distribution of the film in America impossible. Lions Gate, with whom I had been in negotiation for almost six months, wanted every single Nike logo on someone's hat to be cleared and they wanted to employ a large West Coast law firm to legal every piece of footage and then indemnify them against any lawsuits that might crop up. That was impossible to do.

Who in the end released it?
Well, I went to The Roxy, who had released *Kurt and Courtney* under similar circumstances. Unfortunately, they were having financial problems at the time and things got so bad that I remember calling Bill Banning, the head of The Roxy, up at home and saying, 'Why don't you ever call me?' and he said, 'Well, I can't make long-distance calls from my home,' because I guess he hadn't paid his phone bills. I suddenly realized they were totally bankrupt. It was a very depressing release of *Biggie and Tupac* in the US.

Do you think the situation with the release of a film like Biggie and Tupac *would be less likely to arise now, given the popularity of the documentary format?*
Perhaps, but how many documentary films are we talking about in a year? Maybe fifteen. Which isn't that many. It's certainly better than five the year before or ten the year before that, but it still means you've got to make a film at a particular level and on a particular subject matter to ensure that it's going to happen. Michael Moore's three films, *Roger and Me* (1989), *Bowling for Columbine* (2002) and *Fahrenheit 9/11* (2004) have all been incredibly successful. He's probably someone people will take risks with, but I'm not sure that that will necessarily apply to the whole field. I think the other thing with Michael's films, which is why they're so successful, is that he's very much a polemicist with a very specific point of view. His portraits of society and people are perhaps less concerned with the complications and contradictions, and ask less questions than other documentary films. Don't get me wrong; I like his work and admire Michael enormously.

I think you're right. I think that there's an appetite and it coincides with a time when TV stations like Channel Four, which are supposed to present in-depth aspects of different kinds of society, have kind of reneged on it. People are looking more to documentaries to get that information. There's an awareness in people that there's this big complicated world out there that they don't understand, and a lot of the connections that might help them understand it are no longer being offered to them by television. This is perhaps even more the case in America, and I certainly think documentary films are filling that void.

What does it say in Collins English Dictionary?
It says, 'Documentary: Being or consisting of documents contained or certified in writing presented or based on factual material. Documentary broadcast films present a factual account of a person or topic using a variety of techniques . . .'

Notes
1. www.nickbroomfield.com.
2. The American Civil Liberties Union.
3. *Who Killed Kurt Cobain?* Halperin, Ian and Wallace, Max (Blake Publishing Ltd, 2002). The authors also recently published *Love and Death: The Murder of Kurt Cobain*, Halperin, Ian and Wallace, Max (Allison & Busby Ltd, 2004).
4. Quartet Books Ltd, 1998.
5. For regular updates on the lawsuit for the wrongful death of Christopher Wallace, visit http://www.allhiphop.com/hiphopnews/?ID=3322.

7

Rough Justice

Aileen Wuornos: The Selling of a Serial Killer, Aileen: The Life and Death of a Serial Killer

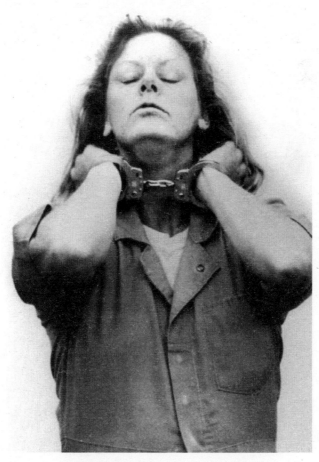

Aileen Wournos awaiting execution,
Aileen: The life and Death of a Serial Killer

Broomfield's initial film on what the American media frenziedly dubbed its first female serial killer revolves around three central characters: prostitute Aileen Wuornos, whom Broomfield interviews in prison whilst charged with the murder of seven of her clients (despite strong evidence to suggest that she acted in self-defence in at least one of the cases), Arlene Pralle, a born-again Christian and adoptive mother of Aileen, and Steve Glazer, an inexperienced lawyer charged with heading Aileen's defence. After Aileen was coerced into entering a plea of no-contest by Pralle and Glazer, multiple death sentences swiftly followed. Raising a number of questions concerning official corruption and the American justice system, Aileen Wuornos: The Selling of a Serial Killer *also looks at the 'Son of Sam' law and the commercial melee that ensued in the fight to exploit Aileen Wuornos and use her name for personal financial gain.*

Having kept in touch with Aileen Wuornos in the intervening twelve years whilst she was on death row awaiting execution, Broomfield found himself subpoenaed to appear at Aileen's final state appeal. Suddenly announcing that she had in fact killed all the men in cold blood, Aileen found herself being sped towards her execution by state governor Jeb Bush. Broomfield's resulting film, Aileen: The Life and Death of a Serial Killer, *examines Aileen's wretched childhood in Troy, Michigan, where she suffered almost unrelenting abuse and violence, an abuse that continued in her years on the road as a hitch-hiking prostitute. Feeling Broomfield to be the one person in whom she can confide, Aileen admits in an unguarded moment that she acted in self-defence but wishes to die to escape the tortuous mental and physical conditions imposed by death row. In her final interview before execu-*

tion, it is apparent that Aileen's mental state has deteriorated, making the decision to execute somebody of unsound mind even more barbarous. A powerful statement against the death penalty and the travesties of the American justice system, Broomfield's most recent work also provides a sympathetic insight into a deeply troubled soul.

JW: *I understand that* Aileen Wuornos: The Selling of a Serial Killer *developed out of a commission you were offered, looking at different serial killers. Most of the serial killers were male and you were interested in Aileen because she was female.*

NB: Channel Four does a number of their films through quite big companies. One of them was contemplating a series of films about serial killers and I looked through the material. I wasn't interested in doing it; it was kind of what you expect and I think it would have been pretty awful. But the thing that caught my eye was this mention of Aileen Wuornos, who was the only woman contender for being a serial killer. She was very defiant and in all the other cases it had been men murdering mainly prostitutes. She was a refreshing change in that it was a prostitute murdering her male clients. Just on the off chance I called up her lawyer in Florida and said what would it take to interview her, and he immediately asked for $30,000.

Was this Steve Glazer?
Correct. And that, in a sense, made me more interested than anything. He sounded kind of nutty on the phone, but I was also amazed that he could be so bold, you know, 'Thirty thousand dollars and you've got the interview.' And I thought the film should really be to do with the commercialization of crime and violence. It was also a surprise because the Son of Sam law had just been passed, prohibiting people from benefiting from their crimes in a commercial way, writing books and so on, and yet here was a lawyer who was clearly benefiting from it. So that seemed to be the basis of the subject and for doing it in a different way. I didn't have to do a head-on study about a serial killer; it was more the phenomenon of the serial killer and what that represented. So I went over to Florida, to Gainesville, where Steve Glazer was based, and was even more amazed to find he didn't have a legal office or even a fax machine. He also had a minimum of training and had mainly represented dope dealers; coincidentally, he had a healthy appetite for dope himself. He liked us because we represented the ticket

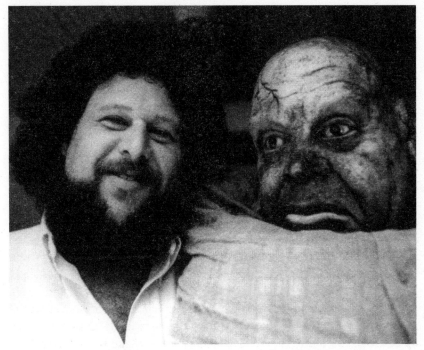

Steve Glazer, Aileen's lawyer with 'Radar' one of his home-made
monster creations, *Aileen: Life and Death of a Serial Killer*

to three meals per day, despite the fact he'd just had an operation on
his stomach to reduce the size of it. He had an incredibly healthy
appetite and a large portion of our budget went into feeding him at the
best restaurants in town. That was really how the film developed – it
was much more a sort of Tom Wolfe approach to the people surrounding Aileen Wuornos.

I was also looking at the American legal system through someone
like Steve Glazer, who was completely unsuited to representing anybody, least of all someone who's about to be executed. In this country
you would have had two barristers and a solicitor working on it and a
sizeable legal team. In America the notion of justice doesn't seem to be
a consideration.

So was Steve Glazer assigned to her?
He wasn't assigned. He was somebody that Aileen's adoptive mother
Arlene Pralle had chosen. Steve had originally secured the adoption of

Aileen Wuornos to Arlene, a born-again Christian who felt Aileen should plead no contest to the charges so that she could get closer to God. And Steve Glazer was a lawyer who was prepared to go along with that.

Arlene Pralle was quite a piece of work.
She was a confused Christian, attention-seeking, horrible, opportunistic person and, I think, genuinely screwy as hell.

There's a scene in the film where Arlene denies you an interview, even though you've paid her for it, and you angrily brand her a very 'deceptive and manipulative woman'. Do you think her reasons for adopting Aileen were to do with Christian ethics or do you think she also saw Aileen as a meal ticket?
I think she genuinely believed Christ had chosen her to somehow save Aileen Wuornos. But Christ seems to enable people to do the craziest things in the world. I think Aileen was so starved of attention and affection and desperate for any kind of support she could find – as are so many people on Death Row – that she kind of falls into Arlene's arms.

Aileen's adoptive mother Arlene Pralle

Aileen at this moment didn't have a family and was alienated from her half-brother and half-sister. She had no real connection with her real mother Diane Wuornos, her father Leo had committed suicide, her brother was dead and so she was a sitting duck for this sort of thing and, I think, went along with it out of a desperate emotional need.

Steve Glazer, whom you state in the second Aileen *film that you liked, comes across as a shyster but also a bit of a lovable rogue. Do you think his motives in the case were purely manipulative?*
I think he was trying to make a name for himself more than anything. He wanted the limelight, he wanted to be an entertainer; he'd originally gone to Las Vegas to try and make his mark in show business with his guitar, playing and sleeping in his car when the money ran out. When he failed at that, he realized the next best thing – and probably the most practical solution – was to study law. He wasn't unintelligent and he's got a good mind, but he didn't have the discipline or the hard-work ethic to be a lawyer. With the Aileen case he didn't have to do much work; he just had to plead no contest for her. He also enjoyed the media attention that the case brought him, the kind of attention he would have got if he'd been a bit more successful as a singer in Las Vegas. I don't think that Steve Glazer was a wicked guy. It was almost an emotional need to have some kind of recognition.

Is there any possibility that Aileen could still be alive today if she'd had a better lawyer? The most harrowing scene in the film is where you show her in the witness stand talking about the Richard Mallory murder, where she was savagely raped and beaten, and it seems patently obvious that it was self-defence. Even one of the jurors afterwards admits that self-defence was likely.
It was complicated. Trisha Jenkins – who was her first lawyer and the public defender – was a very good lawyer who had a strong legal team around her. But she had inherited the case about a month before the trial because Aileen had dismissed her very first lawyer, who again had been trying to sell her story to Hollywood. Trisha Jenkins had taken on the case but didn't really have enough time to do the research into the backgrounds of the murders and asked for a continuance, which was refused. The original presiding judge was a female but the prosecution appealed against her, claiming that she might be biased because of her sex. Subsequently, an older judge, known as the 'Hanging

Judge', was brought out of retirement. He was totally in bed with the prosecution right from the beginning and refused to allow Trisha Jenkins the time really to research the background of people like Mallory. The judge also, somewhat unusually, agreed for evidence of the other six murders to be introduced into the Richard Mallory trial. Trisha Jenkins was given the wrong social-security number and wrong driver's licence number for Mallory, the murder victim, meaning that when she did background checks she didn't realize that he had a long history of sexual crimes and had served time for rape and sexual abuse. None of Mallory's previous history emerged during the first trial, and after receiving the death sentence I think Aileen was very disenchanted with Trisha Jenkins. Aileen had a short fuse and if she felt somebody had let her down she'd just dismiss them. This is what she did to Trisha Jenkins, much against everyone's advice.

By this time Aileen had semi-fallen in love with Arlene Pralle and went along with her wishes. When Steve Glazer was appointed to represent her, he didn't even bother picking up the files and paperwork on the case from Trisha Jenkins' office. For all we know, all that material is probably still there, so all the background information and research that a lawyer would normally do was never looked at. So to answer your question, yes, I think she could be alive today and I know that Trisha Jenkins had already plea-bargained on five of the murders. I think there were valid grounds for appeal on the Richard Mallory case, which was probably the case that she was actually executed on. But that never happened, and you could say that Steve and Arlene together, in conjunction with Aileen's unbalanced mental state, are responsible for her not being with us today. It's a secondary question, whether life would have been much better in an institution for the criminally insane, which is probably where Aileen would have ended up. But what the film really addresses is the question of justice and what kind of example we set when we execute someone like Aileen and what kind of message that sends out.

I think that's the central tenet of the second film, Aileen: The Life and Death of a Serial Killer. *From the first film, I was left with the overriding sense of Aileen Wuornos as a commodity whose story is to be bought and sold. This is what also seems to cause Aileen herself the most chagrin.*
Aileen had never really managed to make any real money in her life. She'd tried to have a steam-clean business and various other things

and it was always a disaster; the only way she ever made any money was by giving blowjobs to guys on the freeway. And so she was really mortified when she realized that the police and everybody else were financially benefiting from her situation.

I think that what hurt her most was not the fact that she wasn't going to be making the money, but how all the people closest to her very quickly betray her. Even her lover Tyria Moore betrays her to the FBI. Do you think she related to you because she got the impression that you wouldn't betray her?
The way that Aileen dealt with life was to be defiant and aggressive. Every time she was let down she became more aggressive and more defiant and she just sort of moved on to the next person or the next situation. Most people who had interviewed her in the past weren't thinking of questions but wanted to hear details of the murders and would make a kind of quasi-moral statement out of her story. I think that Aileen sensed that I listened to her because I just wanted to know about her and her life. We'd also had this incident where we'd been arrested at the prison before the interview for breaking the rules about what could be filmed on the prison grounds. It got around the institution that we'd been arrested at the back of the prison and our car was being searched, and Aileen thought this was hilarious and so liked us for that too. And then the prison wouldn't actually allow us to go back in and do a second interview after the chief warden refused to allow us back in. The fact that we were also being messed around by the system was, I'm sure, another aspect about us that Aileen related to.

You mention to Aileen that Arlene was also being obstructive to you. I think this also acted as a bond.
Perhaps, but I also think that because I had spent much more time with Steve and Arlene at that point than she had, I was also a source of news for her. I knew a lot about her life and the people she was closest to, so I think she was very interested in me from that point of view as well. And then after the interview she quite often wrote to me and used to do these funny little drawings of herself in the prison and I think, in a way, she projected a lot of the things she thought we were. She thought we were members of a rock band playing in the prison later that evening, and we kept saying, 'We're not.'

Why would she have thought that?
God knows. Maybe because we got arrested. She projected the fact that we were always out partying and having a great time, which is obviously what she wanted to be doing. When the film came out Aileen heard from her best friend Dawn that she had come out very well in it. People warmed to her and it was felt that we'd pretty much put her attitude about the cops and stuff across. Because of the first film, a lot of people, like the Coalition of Lawyers in New York and other civil rights groups, all tried to represent Aileen and get an appeal for the first murder. But Aileen was so suspicious of people that she just fell out with them all.

In that first interview she does place a heavy kind of responsibility on you because she asks you actually to go out and investigate the case.
That happened over the next twelve years. In the intervening time there were people like Phyllis Chesler and various lawyer groups who contacted me, and I put them in touch with Aileen Wuornos to try and do precisely that. I think that as a film-maker you're in a better position to act as a catalyst to galvanize experts into action. These experts are far better at carrying out investigations into what really happened contractually between the police and CBS than I am. I worked with those groups and tried to move things forward over a period of two or three or four years. But it all broke down. There was also a lawyer from this country who went to the jail to have several meetings with Aileen, but each of those ended in arguments, fallings out and more mistrust on Aileen's part. I think there was a window of opportunity when things could have changed if only Aileen had trusted anybody at this stage of her life. Arlene Pralle was certainly against all this as it interfered with her vision of what she wanted for Aileen, which was to repent and come clean with God. I suppose Arlene was the person who was giving Aileen more love and support and strength than anyone else at this stage, but Aileen was surely a terrible judge of people.

When you earlier mentioned that Aileen had fallen in love with Arlene, did you mean in a platonic or sexual way?
I don't know that there was an overt sexual thing, but there was certainly an undercurrent. There was a sort of wacky, semi-sexual, semi-mystical religious concept going on. Their relationship existed on a very weird level, but then I think a lot of Aileen's emotions existed on

that level. She was in love with Tyria, who betrayed her right through to the very end and to her execution. So I don't think someone like Aileen can be judged on a normal, rational level. I don't think she operated like that.

Aileen is so hurt and angered by the fact that the American justice system doesn't seem to be interested in the self-defence aspect at all, protesting that they're interested only in the amount of people that she's killed to see if she qualifies as a serial killer.

The prosecutor on the Richard Mallory case, John Tanner, was a strange guy. I think he genuinely hated women and certainly hated prostitutes because he felt that prostitutes were these Jezebels who had been sent down to sap man's physical and moral strength. He also felt that prostitutes were really evil people who only felt good about themselves when they were controlling men and that prostitutes generally hated men and were vengeful. Tanner believed Aileen Wuornos to be an extreme example of this. He had also been Ted Bundy's spiritual advisor when he was in prison and had actually campaigned to delay and prevent the execution of Ted Bundy, who for some reason he had really identified with. Ted Bundy mainly killed prostitutes. Tanner was very skilled at soliciting mass-media coverage and propagated the notion of Aileen being some kind of predator, living off the blood of the men she had killed like a vampire. He was largely responsible for the idea that she was pure evil, a Christian way of thinking that avoided looking at what might have created this person or what it was in her background that upset her and made her as violent and irrational as she was. And that was a position that was very much taken up by the press, who were quick to paint Aileen as this man-hating lesbian serial killer.

Governor Jeb Bush – who, with his brother President George, has a reputation for executions – quickly realized that this was a widely held perception and that his execution of her would get him a lot of support, particularly as he was up for re-election in November. All these elements fatally came together.

Before her mental health deteriorates, Aileen is perceptive in recognizing that she's been given all these death sentences for purely political purposes and the fact that her crimes take a backseat to the election hopes of people like Jeb Bush.

Aileen Wuornos as a child

She's a very intelligent woman and so much of what she says – in fact, nearly *everything* she says – is right. You just get flashes of that paranoia and that violence which I'm sure culminated in those murders. A lot of the time what she says is absolutely true and absolutely spot on in terms of how she sees all those people who have lived off her and abused her even further, including Jeb Bush and the cynical way in which he used the system to have her executed when it suited him.

Also clear from the first film is that after Tyria Moore gives evidence against Aileen she is offered immunity from prosecution. This is interesting given that a lot of the witnesses quite clearly identify her as being with Aileen at the time of a number of the killings.

Aileen Wuornos in 1992

Tyria was certainly aware of the Richard Mallory murder, which was the first one. I think she was also completely aware that all these gifts that Aileen was giving her were from the murdered victims. But she was given protection, made a state witness and was part of the movie-rights package that the police were making. I think the trade-off was that if she joined the police and worked against Aileen she wouldn't be prosecuted, even though she was an accessory to murder.

The second film is obviously more about the death penalty and the barbarity of putting someone to death who is quite clearly insane, but what were your views on the death penalty and capital punishment at this point?

I was always anti-death penalty. I've always believed that you don't gain anything by violence or killing people. Violent acts and killing people only produces more violent acts and more killing, and I think if you're trying to give an example that killing is not the appropriate way of behaving, then executing someone certainly doesn't achieve that. I was aware of all that, but it really hit home when I was taken on a tour of the electric chair. You see the bars of soap at the bottom of the shower which were all used by the last prisoners just before they were executed and you see the chair on which they are shaved. All the stuffing is coming out of the chair, and when I asked the jailer why he didn't get a new one, he said, 'Oh, no, we like them to feel the itching of the stuffing coming out of the chair so they know they've come as low as they can go.' You realize there is a vindictiveness and vengeance about it that's so unhealthy. Nothing comes up but more hatred and more vengeance and more weird things. It's that kind of mentality that has got us into the situation in Abu Ghraib and other American prisons.

There isn't this belief that there are certain inalienable rights no matter what just by virtue of one being another human being and that these rights are to be respected more than anything else. The latest, almost biblical thinking in parts of America gives this very primitive sense of justice which runs right through the legal system. In a democracy, you look for a system that is fair and is equal and is not based exclusively on how big a lawyer you can get; that there is a system that really wants to get to the bottom of the truth and wants to give everyone a real opportunity to present their story in the best possible light. This is absolutely not what happened in Aileen Wuornos's case, and that was probably the most upsetting thing about it.

Just to fast-forward a little bit, I understand that when you had made the first Aileen film, Channel Four hated it – I think those are your words, 'Hated it'. What was it that they were displeased about?
It was quite surprising because I was cutting it in California, and Riete Oord was out there as well. It was the same team that I used on *The Leader, His Driver* and on *Tracking Down Maggie*, Riete Oord and Barry Ackroyd, and while we were doing the edit we'd sent a rough cut back to Peter Moore, who was the commissioning editor. I liked Peter Moore a great deal, but he's got quite strong opinions and sometimes, like a lot of commissioning editors, he hasn't actually had that much experience as a film-maker. He has the best possible intentions

though. I remember him saying that he thought we were on drugs. He sent me this fax in the days before fax paper was cut and I remember coming down in the morning and there was this incredibly long fax right across the living room floor from Peter Moore claiming that he thought we were on drugs.

Why did he think that?
He thought the cut was so bad and felt that we would be slaughtered by feminists who read *Time Out*. He felt that we should use experts in feminism to give their opinions. He wanted me to pull the film from the London Film Festival, where it was due to be screened; it subsequently developed into an unpleasant argument. I felt that we'd made the film that represented our experience and didn't really understand how one would use an expert who wasn't a part of the film or a part of the process. It wasn't that kind of film. I think that it is dangerous to start introducing arbitrary characters because there's no natural boundary once you start doing that. I remember saying, 'OK, well, if I pull it out of the film festival I'll be making a statement as to why I'm pulling it out. And I'm going to hand you all the footage and I'd be very interested to see what film you come out with.'

You've not had much luck with film festivals.
Anyway, Peter backed down and was apologetic, but it still made for a pretty unpleasant edit. I remember him really hating it when I was shouting at Arlene Pralle and calling her manipulative and deceptive. Maybe he was being protective of me and for that reason felt that it should be taken out of the film.

But surely deception and manipulation are at the crux of the film.
But it is an ugly scene and I certainly do lose my temper and am not the most attractive person at that moment, but I felt it was part of the film and that it should stay in. In a sense, you can't just keep pulling everything out.

And, of course, the film went on to win the Royal Television Society Award. A source of vindication?
Yeah. I think it won the Grierson too. To be honest, those awards never mean very much.

I was looking at the way you display them.
They're all over the shop, but I guess it's an affirmation in some form or other.

Oddly enough, the edit on the second Aileen film was difficult too because the film was shot in two parts. We had one cut up to June and then I went back to the US on two occasions to interview Aileen and to go to her hometown and then back again for the execution. We had to substantially recut the film each time. Claire Ferguson, the editor, did a great job.

The second film goes into more detail about Aileen's background to explain why some of the atrocities may have happened. It talks about her father, who committed suicide in prison where he was sent after sodomizing a little boy, and also looks more closely at the extent to which Aileen was demonized by the media and by the American public. You even have a clip of somebody calling her a 'man-hating lesbian hooker', and the hatred is so intense. Was any aspect of Aileen's cause taken up by any feminist bodies?
Phyllis Chesler and the National Coalition for Lawyers were feminists and were the women who were trying to get an appeal for the Richard Mallory case. Trisha Jenkins, Aileen's first lawyer, was a very strong supporter of those issues. But Aileen fell out with everybody and didn't see herself as a feminist or a lesbian. As one coalition member put it, 'It depends what day you ask her.' Aileen could also not see why the coalition would find her case important politically. In fact, in the spring of 1991, Chesler persuaded attorney Leonard Weinglass to agree to defend Wuornos *pro bono* if Chesler could raise fifty thousand dollars but . . .

Aileen didn't want to harness this support?
No, she didn't. For one reason or another.

And what were the circumstances that led towards your going back and making Aileen: The Life and Death of a Serial Killer?
Well, I was subpoenaed. They were going to show aspects of the first film, the sequence showing Steve Glazer smoking dope on his way to visit Aileen in prison, to show that she'd really had completely inadequate legal representation and that there should be an appeal on those grounds. So I was subpoenaed. I was in the middle of shooting *Biggie*

and Tupac. Joan and I went down to Florida and we had all the equipment with us. I thought I might as well do an update, particularly as it became apparent as soon as we got down there that the whole thing was just a sham. Basically, the decision had been made to execute Aileen. This was just some kind of *pro forma* thing that they were going through and they weren't really examining any mitigating information or evidence that was actually going to cause a retrial.

There is that sequence they show from the first film, with Steve Glazer making the 'seven-joint ride' to the prison. The prosecution accuses you of manipulating the footage because, at the start of the journey, Steve is wearing an old green T-shirt, but on arriving at the prison he is wearing a white shirt. It seems fairly obvious to me that he simply changed his shirt on the way.
That's right. He simply arrived at the prison and put a clean shirt on. I think that that prosecutor was worried that my film might actually upset his plan to get Aileen executed and that there might be an appeal on the basis that Steve Glazer was not only legally incompetent, but he was on drugs at the time when he was giving his client advice.

He was trying to discredit not only your integrity but also your film too.
He was trying to discredit the film and it was unfortunate in a sense that I didn't really know what bits of the film were going to be used as evidence. Had I known I would have found all that out-take footage and actually shown it. I remember now, of course, that Steve went into the toilets in a restaurant and changed his shirt before going to see Aileen, which makes perfect sense because we were in that car for about seven hours and he looked a bloody mess in that green T-shirt. He wouldn't want to go into prison as a lawyer looking like he'd just got out of bed.

And what about this whole issue of a film-maker's right to play around with chronology and present factual evidence in a creative way?[1]
The most important thing is to believe what you're saying is correct. I don't think you can change the meaning of something, otherwise you're a propagandist and not a film-maker as such. The evidence you present has to be accurate and you can't make a piece of footage say something that is against what it inherently means or give it an addi-

tional meaning that wasn't there in the first place. That's not what documentary is there for.

Let's talk about your relationship with Aileen in the twelve years between the first film and the second. How did it change through that time? How did you feel, even before you had gone back to re-interview her, about her state of mind?
I had written to Aileen intermittently and I guess I'd been much more in touch with Dawn Botkins, who was her best friend. During our phone conversations Dawn always very respectfully called me 'Mr Broomfield' and I think really believed in me because she loved the first film so much. I never met Dawn, but I felt that I knew her so well. When I did finally meet her, she looked completely different from what I'd imagined. Dawn wrote to Aileen every morning for a couple of hours and every conversation I had with her would relate to Aileen. So it was quite a good way of staying in touch with Aileen and also finding out what Aileen's mental condition was like, what she was thinking about and what was going on in her life.

Obviously I offered to help Aileen in any way I could, either in trying to get legal representation or saying something on her behalf. That was why her appeal lawyer, Joe Hobson, got in touch with me and asked if I would be prepared to be a witness. I said, 'Sure.' And then the prosecutor, whose name I can't remember, called me up and asked if I would be available to make some statements at the Florida appeal.

There's obviously a change in Aileen. Instead of wanting to prove that she acted in self-defence, the endless trials and retrials cause her to decide that she wants to die.
At first . . . I don't know what Aileen was thinking. I think she actually thought she was going to live with Arlene Pralle down on their horse ranch, and when she realized that wasn't going to happen and that no matter what she pleaded she would be incarcerated, she decided then that it was a lost cause. I think deep inside her she believed for one reason or another that she'd acted in self-defence. And who knows what those reasons are. Aileen certainly thought that she was so wronged that perhaps this was justifiable. But I certainly found it interesting that whilst interviewing her she could get so outraged over very simple misunderstandings and statements that I'd made that she didn't agree with. There was a total violence and craziness and you

could see it wasn't like a normal person. You could see how she could probably argue herself into anything and that the murders had come out of that kind of thinking and that sort of behaviour. I felt that Aileen really believed that she acted in self-defence but that this was never going to be recognized in a court of law and so she was never going to get out. I think at that point she decided she wanted to die.

It's another question as to whether or not someone who doesn't have the right to make a single decision when they're in prison, can't even have breakfast when they want to and can't even write a letter without it being vetted should have the decision over whether or not they stay alive. It seems a complete contradiction if you're saying, 'Somebody who is completely unsafe to make any decisions at all needs to be guarded twenty-four hours a day.' What are you doing asking them if they want to take their own life or not? It just doesn't make any sense. So I think the bigger question is not really whether Aileen wanted to stay alive or not but what our justice system feels is appropriate for someone who is clearly mentally unstable. Do we think life should be taken away or not? It's kind of hypocritical to say it's Aileen's decision because she could make decisions in other areas of her life but none of them would be acted on. It just suited Jeb Bush and the justice system, who wanted to execute her to say, 'Well, this is what she wants.'

And that's the main thrust of the film, isn't it? You passionately state to the rows of news crews your belief that America is about to execute a woman who is clearly insane.
I think that America has a very, very primitive justice system. It's the only country that until relatively recently was still executing juveniles. There was a fourteen-year-old boy who was executed who was so small that the helmet wouldn't stay on his head. There was another prisoner who was so mentally retarded that he said he was going to leave the other half of his last meal for when he came back. There are endless stories like that about the inequities of the system. There were cases where a person was so psychotic they said, 'Oh well, we'll give them drugs so that they're not psychotic at the time that they're executed.' All these horrendous examples give a portrait of a completely barbaric legal system.

Channel Four decided to advertise the film's broadcast by a slightly

gleefully ghoulish approach, with a pull-out ad in the Guardian *that had a picture of you with the words 'The last person that got this close she murdered.'*

I objected to that. I said that I thought it was in really bad taste, that it was sensationalistic and was exactly not what the film was about. I remember they called me up saying that they were doing a good job, they're the best people in the business and this is what the public want – sort of, 'Stop being difficult.' I mean, they didn't say that, but it was like, 'Let us do our job. All we're trying to do is promote your film, so work with us.' I thought it was really cheap and it made me uncomfortable.

The upside, I guess, is that the film had huge viewing figures when it did air on TV.

I think it was three and a half million up to midnight. That is really good, so in other ways they did a good job.

Let's talk about the final interview with Aileen. What were your thoughts going into it knowing this was the last time you were going to speak to her, and how far had her mental state deteriorated by this point? She starts to talk about the radiation being used to control her brain.

I felt going into the interview that this was her opportunity to set the record straight. I was hoping that she would go into the details of some of the murders and that she'd talk about what was going through her head at the time and really clarify whether they were all in self-defence. And it seemed that this was the time that she would do it or else she would never do it as she was going to be executed in the morning. What I hadn't really accounted for was that Aileen was so determined to be executed that she felt that if she'd said something it might change the execution.

She point-blank refuses to talk about the self-defence issue.

Yes, because she thought this might influence the execution. What she really wanted to talk about was the crooked cops. She wanted the film to very much go in that direction, to investigate the cops. And she then came up with a lot of quite strange assertions, that they were surveying her from the sky and that they were controlling her mind in various ways, and I felt like I sort of had to push it a bit. After all, this was the last opportunity to move the interview to some kind of conclusion in terms of her state of mind at the time of the murders, whether she was delusional or not. I didn't realize that mentioning her biological mother was going to bring on such an incredible outburst, I really didn't.

Her mother Diane had asked for Aileen's forgiveness.
Yeah, and I thought, in a way, asking her for forgiveness might be of some solace to Aileen. She would think, 'Oh well, at least my mum wants to make peace and I'll go happier to the execution knowing that.' I didn't realize at all that it was going to upset her. A number of people have chided me for being cruel in mentioning the mother, but I really thought it was going to have the opposite effect. I mean, it certainly would with nearly anyone else.

Why did you shout, 'I'm so sorry,' when she was led away?
Because I felt that the interview was such a disappointment for her. And here she was, cutting it short, having a pretty unpleasant time. Obviously she was disturbed by the fact that she was going to be executed the next day, and, frankly, who wouldn't be? But I felt that maybe she thought that I'd let her down, and it just seemed such a sad way to be saying goodbye to somebody.

You've said in other interviews that you have been unable ever to sit through this interview sequence. Is that still the case?
I certainly wouldn't choose to sit through it. I just felt so . . . seeing her in that last section of the film with those eyes, talking about a raped woman being put to death. It almost becomes sort of biblical . . . doesn't it? And it's hard not to feel the comment is aimed at you.

One of the things that clearly emerges from this film and from the first one is that everyone was colluding to get a film made about her life. What were your thoughts about Monster[2] *and how do you feel it may possibly affect the legacy of Aileen Wuornos's life and death?*
Charlize Theron's performance, which was based on viewing the tapes of my two films, was fantastic. I was dreading seeing a bad performance, something like *Overkill*,[3] with Jean Smart as Aileen, which is such a bad film. I really thought Charlize got into her psyche, especially considering that they did the film incredibly quickly. Director

Patty Jenkins took a very simple and economic approach to the material that I thought worked very well. But *Monster* didn't really deal with some of the big issues. It didn't really deal with much of her background and the way in which that had impinged on her behaviour. And I don't think it really dealt with the issue of the justice system and what sort of treatment is appropriate for someone with Aileen's mental condition.

It's also interesting that Christina Ricci played a fictional character as opposed to portraying Aileen's lover Tyria Moore.
I guess they had legal problems with the name. It's very hard to distance myself from the real Tyria Moore and look at the character played by Christina Ricci and really support it because I don't think Christina Ricci was anything like Tyria. Not only did she not look like Tyria Moore, but she didn't behave like the Tyria Moore that I knew.

Nearly all the articles on Monster *deflected attention back to your films. John Patterson in the* Guardian *urged people to seek them out.*[4]
Obviously, from the beginning when Charlize called up wanting to get the tapes, I had the choice of either working with them and trying to make it into a positive experience that would help both films and an understanding of Aileen, or to say, 'Fuck off, I've done all this work, I'm not going to share it with you.' And I'm pleased I did what I did, which is to send them a rough cut of the second film, which was more generous than I needed to be. I think we actually did benefit from each other and, in a way, the films authenticated Charlize's performance. The films fed off each other.

We are coming to an end now. One of the things that I think has emerged clearly is the fact that you want your films to cause change. I've heard another interview where you've said you don't feel that the second Aileen Wuornos film did this because the only thing that really came out of it was Aileen's execution. Do you still feel the same way?
Well, in her immediate case, yes. I think that the film has contributed to the debate about the death penalty. It's probably cast some shadow over politicians like Governor Jeb Bush who are prepared to use somebody's execution to try and curry favour with voters who hold those kinds of vengeful positions. I hope we'll have more of a debate as to what we really want from our justice system, what kind of example we

should be setting and what sort of representation people on death row should get in terms of legal counsel. And the importance of people in a democracy to believe there is a balanced, fair legal system which is not dependent on your income. Whether you're guilty or whether you're innocent should have nothing to do with what your annual income is. It shouldn't be to do with what kind of lawyer you can afford. That is not what democracy is about and the film raises all those issues. I think, probably with the help of *Monster*, a lot of people who wouldn't normally watch the film have watched it because in America they're packaged to go together. They were released together by Blockbuster.

On the piece that followed the television broadcast of Aileen: The Life and Death of a Serial Killer *you describe it as the most disturbing and personal film you have ever made, partly because you got to know Aileen over a twelve-year period and began making the film as a witness and then ended up attending her execution. Because of this, you said that the film gives you nightmares. Is this still the case?*
I haven't been having the dreams, but I had them for a long time afterwards. I probably had them for about six months after I'd finished the shoot. In a way, it was quite good for me. It was a very painful experience but I think I ended up making a very compassionate film which got a fantastic reaction from the audience. A lot of people were really moved and touched by the film and it opened me up as a person. It was very painful; I think it's a sensitive film about someone whom it would have been very easy not to have been sensitive about. That's precisely what an audience most identifies with.

Notes
1. 'The pitfall for Moore is not subjectivity but accuracy. We expect him to hold an opinion and argue it, but we also require his facts to be correct. I was an admirer of *Bowling for Columbine* until I discovered that some of his "facts" were wrong, false or smudged.' Roger Ebert, 'Politicians in the Doc', *The Times*, 8 July 2004.
2. Directed by Patty Jenkins and employing a surprisingly non-sensationalist style, *Monster* opened to largely positive reviews and brought Charlize Theron a Best Actress Academy Award for her performance as Aileen Wuornos.
3. Directed by Peter Levin, *Overkill: The Aileen Wuornos Story* was a salacious TV movie.
4. 'In the end, Broomfield and Churchill's search for truth inevitably trumps

Jenkins' fictionalisation.' John Patterson, *Guardian*, Friday 23 January 2004. For information on the life and death of Aileen Wuornos and her court case visit: http://www.crimelibrary.com/notorious_murders/women/wuornos/new_ch. html?sect=11.

8

Broomfield and Son 2

Last Words

Following in the family tradition: Barney Broomfield's
Welcome to the Real World

JW: *I'm intrigued to see the documentary film that your son Barney has made. Is it titled yet, by the way?*
NB: It's called *Welcome to the Real World*.

That takes me right back to the start of the book and your father Maurice telling you that you were going to have to go and get a job.
Well, it's what I say to him in the film, so history repeats itself.

You worked with Barney on Biggie and Tupac, *on which he was an executive producer. Is a move into documentary film-making something you've encouraged him to do and how do you feel about the Broomfield film-making dynasty continuing through Barney?*
Well, it's a wonderful way of life and it gives you the opportunity to meet lots of very different people and find out about different societies and communities. Maybe it's that aspect that is the most appealing thing about it and which enables you to integrate all your interest into it. It's a pathway to anything that you're interested in, whether it's politics, music, religion, psychology or whatever. You can go there. Barney's first reaction was, 'And I'm I getting paid for doing it?' That's a fantastic thing; you are paid to absorb something and make it into your passion.

And is this the way you still feel about it today?
Absolutely. I think I need to play around with making films in other ways and explore other forms as well. I've still yet to make a successful . . . well, I wouldn't say fiction film, but a film that is more scripted, more thought out; this is something that I'd like to try and do.

Have you got any specific ideas at the moment?
I'm loath to talk about it in too much detail in case it never happens. I am thinking of doing something about foreign workers in England; more particularly, looking at all the ways in which they're exploited whilst everyone sits back and pretends that they don't know it's happening, and how our economy totally depends on these people.

And this is one you think you'd do as more of a scripted piece as opposed to a documentary?
I think I'd do it more as a scripted piece, but very much based on facts and things that are actually happening.

And what other subjects would you like to tackle in a documentary piece?
There would be an endless list of those. One of the things that is wonderful about documentaries and documentary film-makers is that they don't seem to grow old. I've talked about Wiseman, Leacock, Pennebaker, the Maysles, etc., and they all keep such a fascination and youthful interest in everything. They're so young at heart. And this is, obviously, really appealing. Their spirits are so young and enquiring, and they're so fascinated by everything and everybody they meet. It's like everything is a delicacy to be savoured and understood. I think it's just a way of being, it's a way of living your life.

Alongside a plethora of other leading documentary film-makers, you were asked for Imagining Reality: The Faber Book of Documentary *the question, 'What is it that you try to achieve most in your documentaries?' Your response at the time was 'To communicate to the audience my own fascination for the subject to the audience.'[1] Would this be the same answer you would give today?*
I think it would. By 'fascination' I mean why I think the subject is significant and why it is significant to an audience. It has to be important enough to devote a huge amount of time to. It's very easy for people to forget why they are making the film sometimes because they have spent so long getting it off the ground that the subject has almost become second nature to them. It is incredibly important to remind the audience of why you think it is so important, because it is often that explanation that makes it relevant to them.

I think you have become, whether you care to admit it or not, very much a touchstone figure, especially for British documentarists. Is this a position you're happy to adopt? In every article about documentaries I read now, Nick Broomfield is always mentioned.[2]

Well, I've always liked being able to encourage young talent to take it up and to demystify it. A lot of people view it like this secret and inaccessible form to get into, and it's actually very straightforward. And I hope that one of the things that will come out of this book, as well as the box sets,[3] is that people in a sense will be able to chart a progression of styles in my work and will see that it's actually quite simple and straightforward. I hope that this will not only answer questions but encourage people to go out and try and tell their own stories. The medium as it is now has become very simple and accessible due to DV cameras, and so there is no reason why people shouldn't communicate their stories. This will inevitably lead to a great richness in terms of the way we'll understand both our culture and the cultures of others. It's always fascinating, and I think there are real opportunities and possibilities to do that now.

I want to conclude on this notion of your need to communicate to an audience your enthusiasm for your subject. Is this still a defining criterion in making the films? Also, what are the things that you hope people will take away from watching your work?

It's all to do with understanding and promoting empathy between one group of people and another. The empathy may well be between people who might not ordinarily have met. I think what these films have – which in a sense no other form has, certainly not straightforward journalism – is an ability to really get into the subjects in depth and to get an understanding of quite complicated issues. It's often the contradictions that are really interesting.

What was really interesting in the Aileen Wuornos films, and in other films too, is that you can't take a black-and-white position on anything. It's seeing how complicated people and issues are; often in newspaper reports you get only a one-sided view as there often isn't time to go into all the convolutions and permutations. You can also get a sense of people's humour and a way of being and speaking that may have drastically changed with time. If you look back at films that were made in the fifties or sixties, you realize that people talked entirely differently then to now. Their whole way of expressing themselves,

of articulating themselves has changed just in that period of time. In a way, you're measuring all of that. Things that you think are everyday and very mundane can take on an incredible significance. I don't think all the films have to be about the most sensational subjects, but they really contribute to our knowledge and understanding.

My last trip was to the Ramallah Film Festival in Palestine; everyone was worried, myself included, that it was going to be life-threatening experience. You'd probably get shot and the whole place would be in disarray, and yet, of course, when you get there you find these wonderfully passionate people who have incredible stories, have a wonderful love for life and are just incredibly hospitable. That very rarely gets properly communicated in a conflict and this is what documentaries can do – get into those people and show that side of things as opposed to just presenting a one-sided view of all Palestinians as suicide bombers. We don't see these incredibly beautiful young Palestinian kids who are so proud to be Palestinian and so rightly upset at the way in which they can't travel anywhere. They can't go to visit the homes of their families because they've been knocked down or closed off in another part of Palestine. You just get a sense of how they're real victims of history and yet their stories are very rarely put across. I think that's what documentary can do and in doing so it can make us a much more sophisticated society.

Notes

1. 'The Burning Question', p. 364.
2. With the release of Michael Moore's *Fahrenheit 9/11* a flurry of articles appeared attempting to discredit Moore's film-making style, the majority of them, including an aforementioned and rather prominent piece by Andrew Anthony titled *Michael and Me*, strongly suggested that Moore had borrowed wholesale from Nick Broomfield.
3. A DVD box set of films with clips from Nick Broomfield's earlier films as well as an historical reel, will be released in Australia, the UK and the US. Films include *Chicken Ranch, Heidi Fleiss, Soldier Girls, Fetishes, Tracking Down Maggie* and *The Leader, His Driver and the Driver's Wife*. The extras will include clips from *Who Cares, Behind the Rent Strike, Soldier Girls* and *Driving Me Crazy*.

Filmography

Who Cares (1970)
Proud to Be British (1973)
Behind the Rent Strike (1974)
Whittingham (1975)
Juvenile Liaison (1976)
Fort Augustus (1976)
Marriage Guidance (1977)
Tattooed Tears (1978)
Soldier Girls (1980)
Chicken Ranch (1982)
Lily Tomlin (1985)
Driving Me Crazy (1988)
Diamond Skulls (1989)
Juvenile Liaison 2 (1990)
The Leader, His Driver and the Driver's Wife (1990)
Monster in a Box (1991)
Too White for Me (1992)
Aileen Wuornos: The Selling of a Serial Killer (1993)
Tracking Down Maggie (1994)
Heidi Fleiss: Hollywood Madam (1995)
Fetishes (1996)
Kurt and Courtney (1997)
Biggie and Tupac (2002)
Aileen: The Life and Death of a Serial Killer (2003)

Please also visit www.nickbroomfield.com to view the series of satirical commercials Broomfield made for the VW Passat.

Bibliography

Books
Allon, Yoram, Cullen, Del and Patterson, Hannah, *Contemporary British and Irish Film Directors: A Wallflower Critical Guide* (Wallflower Press, 2001).
Macdonald, Kevin and Cousins, Mark (Eds), *Imagining Reality: The Faber Book of Documentary* (first edn) (Faber and Faber, 1996).
Pierson, John, *Spike, Mike, Slackers & Dykes: A Guided Tour across a Decade of Independent American Cinema* (Faber and Faber, 1996).
Rothman, William, *Documentary Film Classics* (Cambridge University Press, 1997).

Articles
Anthony, Andrew, 'Michael and Me', *Observer*, Sunday 23 May 2004.
Brooks, Xan, 'Factory Records', *Guardian*, Wednesday 3 March 2004.
Carroll, Rory, 'Terre'Blanche Returns to a New World', *Guardian*, Thursday 10 June 2004.
Curtis, Bryan, 'Honest Tabloid Sleaze: Nick Broomfield and the Art of Trash', http://slate.msn.com/id/2079986.
Davis, Clive, 'Politicians in the Doc', *The Times*, Thursday 8 July 2004.
Gilligan, Beth, 'Making Money: Profits and Ethics in Documentary Filmmaking', http://www.kamera.co.uk/features/making_money_profits_ethics_in_documentary_filmmaking_php.
Longrigg, Clare, 'Sympathy for the She Devil', *Harpers and Queen*, December 2003.

Patterson, John, *Guardian*, Friday 23 January 2004.
Rabin, Nathan, 'Nick Broomfield', http://www.theonionavclub.com/4004/feature1.html.
Smith, Mat, 'Nick Broomfield's Top Five Documentaries', *Arena*, June 2004.

Websites
http://www.nickbroomfield.com
http://www.pennebakerhegedusfilms.com
http://www.zipporah.com (website for Frederick Wiseman)
http://www.britmovie.co.uk

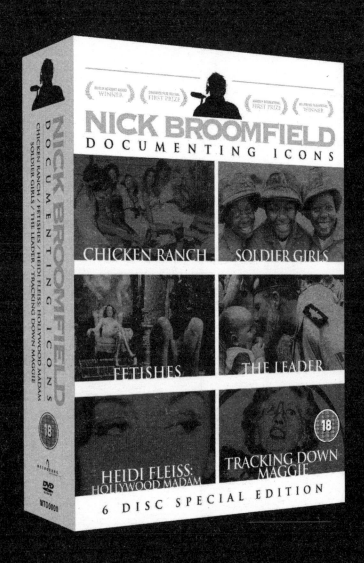